GEORGE C. MARSHALL

General George C. Marshall   (George C. Marshall Research Library)

MAKERS OF AMERICA

GEORGE C. MARSHALL
A GENERAL FOR PEACE

ALAN SAUNDERS

Facts On File, Inc.
AN INFOBASE HOLDINGS COMPANY

To
Scott, Thomas, Katherine, Jason
—and their grandfather,
another soldier for whom Honor and Duty
were always paramount.

George C. Marshall: **A General for Peace**

Copyright © 1996 by Alan Saunders

Facts On File, Inc.
11 Penn Plaza
New York NY 10001

Library of Congress Cataloging-in Publication Data
Saunders, Alan.
    George C. Marshall: a general for peace Alan Saunders.
      p. cm. — (Makers of America)
    Includes bibliographical references.
    Summary: Recounts the life and achievements of the Nobel Peace Prize–winning United States Army general.
    ISBN 0-8160-2666-1 (alk. paper)
    1. Marshall, George C. (George Catlett), 1880–1959—Juvenile literature. 2. Generals—United States—Biography—Juvenile literature. 3. Statesmen—United States—Biography—Juvenile literature. 4. United States. Army—Biography—Juvenile literature. [1. Marshall, George C. (George Catlett), 1880–1959. 2. Generals. 3. Statesmen.] I. Title. II. Series: Makers of America (Facts on File, Inc.)
E745.M37S28 1995
973.918'092—dc20   95–17623
[B]

Text design by Debbie Glasserman

This book is printed on acid-free paper.

Printed in the United States of America

VB FOF 10 9 8 7 6 5 4 3 2 1

CONTENTS

PROLOGUE
PEACE—THIS SOLDIER'S LEGACY

June 5, 1947, Cambridge, Massachusetts. In measured tones, first in Latin and then in English, the president of Harvard University reads the citation, ". . . an American to whom Freedom owes an enduring debt of gratitude, a soldier and statesman whose ability and character brook only one comparison [George Washington] in the history of the nation."

Standing in front of him, the tall, ramrod-straight man remains silent and unsmiling. And then, as James B. Conant finishes, a thunderous ovation bursts from the 8,000 gathered in front of the steps of Madison Memorial in Harvard Yard. With a faint smile, the General of the Army, former special ambassador to China and current U.S. secretary of state George Catlett Marshall accepts the degree of doctor of laws.

General Marshall has not come to Harvard Yard as a conquering hero. . . . He first had to face a hostile congressional inquiry into the unpreparedness at Pearl Harbor, an inquiry during which he shouldered his fair share of the blame.

Then came his failed mission to China. Admittedly, ending the 20-year-old Chinese civil war on terms acceptable to the United States was a nearly hopeless cause from the beginning, but for men like Marshall, the objectives—not the obstacles—are paramount. So for a bitterly frustrating year, Marshall continued his efforts.

Badly in need of nonpartisan help, President Truman had decided to cut his losses. He recalled Marshall to America to serve as secretary of state, the second most important position in the government.

One of Marshall's first tasks at the Department of State was the Foreign Ministers' Conference in Moscow, where the "Big Four" (Britain, France, the U.S.S.R. and the United States) met for six weeks of endless arguments over the future of Europe in general and Germany in particular. Vyacheslav Molotov, the Soviet foreign minister, found most of the Western proposals unacceptable. Disillusioned and angry, Marshall called on Joseph Stalin directly. After 46 meetings it finally became clear to him that a ravaged Continent suited Stalin extremely well, and that Marshall's and America's remaining faith in Soviet goodwill was indeed misplaced.

Yet it is this man, fresh from major defeats and disappointments, that the men and women of Harvard are applauding. And these are not ignorant masses easily led by a charismatic leader but sober representatives of the best-educated, most successful people in America. Many of them have been imbued from the cradle with the thought that service to their country is indeed the highest goal.

And that is one achievement that friend and foe alike recognize in Marshall. Even the ordinary man and woman in the street know that Marshall has put duty and honor before expediency or self-interest. They have seen him struggle with Congress, fight the army bureaucracy, tangle with the president and remain steadfast to his goal—to build an army that could triumph in World War II, and once built, to direct it in the most effective manner. Marshall has won the confidence and trust not only of world leaders, but of the common soldier and citizen as well.

Marshall has a plan in coming to Harvard. Honors do not matter to him. Witness the fact that the university has twice before offered him an honorary degree. Both times he has declined, since Harvard insists he must be present for the occasion. This time it is different. At the State Department, the idea of a plan to resolve the desperate postwar European situation where victors and vanquished alike are mired in unemployment, cold and near famine has been in the works since April.

The Harvard audience does not know that later that afternoon, in a brief and unemotionally delivered speech, Marshall will announce a program designed to guarantee security to America and restore prosperity to a ravaged Europe. That here at Harvard commencement, they will be witnessing the birth of the European Recovery Program, or as most of the world will know it, the Marshall Plan. A plan that in its simplicity still embodies altruism and enlightened self-interest to a degree seldom—if ever—encountered before or since.

And it is not a moment too soon. In Europe conditions are so bad that it is almost difficult to tell who has won and who has

A floral parade in Lisse, Holland, in honor of General Marshall and the Marshall Plan (George C. Marshall Research Library)

lost the war. The British have just announced that they can no longer honor their commitments in the Greek civil war, for they only have enough funds for six months. Even worse off, the French and the Italians fear not only bankruptcy but civil conflict, as their militant Communists become stronger and bolder. Across the Continent inflation and unemployment are rampant. Even nature seems to have turned against Europe. The worst winter in 40 years is followed by a disastrous harvest. Farmers everywhere are feeding their meager crops to their animals rather than risk selling them for worthless currency. The Germans are subsisting on less than half their normal caloric intake. For the first time since the Middle Ages, mass starvation looms as a real possibility across Europe.

At the Moscow conference Marshall has seen how well these conditions serve Stalin's purpose. To thrive, communism must have discontent and hunger on its side, precisely the dominant forces in Europe at the moment.

Were these forces to prevail, Western Europe might fall and the Americas would be isolated from their motherlands and their main markets. Marshall's plan is as untried as it is bold. Rebuild the economies not only of friends, but of foes; as the victor, seek not to plunder but to create.

But back in the United States, there are huge obstacles. The mood is to throw away the uniform, to cut taxes and to return to the cherished dream of an America independent from the rest of the world. It will be Marshall's first task to convince America and Congress that a new day has dawned, that the new Pax Americana, the 20th-century successor to Rome's, carries not only the distinction of the United States being the most powerful nation in the world, but that the honor also has a price.

And he has chosen today, and hallowed Harvard Yard, as the time and place to sound the new crusade's first battle cry.

1

THE EARLY YEARS—AN "INDIFFERENT SCHOLAR"

George Catlett Marshall Junior was born on December 31, 1880 in Uniontown, Pennsylvania; he was the third child of George Catlett Marshall and Laura Bradford Marshall. His father was a prominent businessman. Both his parents hailed from Augusta, Kentucky, but they came from old Virginian stock, a background that included a number of illustrious ancestors.

As a boy, he was what polite Victorian society discreetly called an "indifferent scholar"—what in today's language would be called a slow learner. This pained his father greatly, so much so that some of that pain was regularly transferred to young George's backside. The theory seemed to be that if one could get the boy's bottom to glow, some of that heat might kindle the spark of learning in his brain. But even though energetically delivered, the thrashings failed to have the desired effect.

Many years later, a chuckling George Marshall would largely attribute this problem to the overly strict tutoring of his aunt, Eliza Stuart. This 80-year-old learned lady read the Old Testament in Hebrew, and for some unknown reason, the New Testament in French. For a year, when George was five, she was put in charge of his education. She assumed this task with harsh and relentless perseverance but little understanding—apparently feeling her own thirst for knowledge to be the natural condition for the small boy placed in her charge. She insisted on verbatim recitations—even on Saturday mornings when George's friends could be seen happily playing outside. "She soured me on study," the general recalled—in an understatement typical of the man.

In 1886, at age six, he was enrolled in Miss Thompson's Academy—a local Victorian version of a superprogressive school. Here the conditions were almost exactly the opposite of what he had encountered with his aunt. Students must be allowed to learn at their own pace, according to the headmistress's theory, so few demands were placed on her charges—a condition that, after his formidable aunt's attentions, young George found greatly to his taste. For the next few years, unfettered by any scholarly demands, he thoroughly enjoyed this new, carefree life.

At age 10, because of his father's suddenly declining financial fortunes—the result of poor real estate investments—he was transferred to the local public school. An interview with the principal uncovered the depths of George's blissful ignorance in nearly all subjects. Humiliated and angry, Mr. Marshall let George know in no uncertain terms what he thought of his son's meager accomplishments.

Like many a bright but poorly schooled child, young George covered his own frustration and shame by pretending that his lack of learning was of his own choice.

One early interest, however, was the subject of history. In spite of himself, George developed a liking for the study of the past, and did well in that subject. Marshall Senior was quite fond of taking his young son for walks along the old Braddock Trail, the path taken by General Edward Braddock in his unsuccessful attack on French-held Fort Duquesne, in the days of colonial America. And he told his little son all about the events that took place there. How the attack was repulsed, and how shortly after, Braddock was killed by the French and their Indian allies. Mr. Marshall took his young son to the general's grave, close by the Trail and not far from the Marshall home. Along the way, too, were the ruins of Fort Necessity, where then Colonel George Washington fought the first of his battles in the French and Indian Wars. George undoubtedly saw the pleasure the telling brought his father, a father whose approval of the boy was so often withheld. Since young Marshall enjoyed both the stories and the outings, it is easy to see him becoming involved in history. And it was probably here too that his interest in soldiering was born.

Other school subjects were a different matter. There his performance bordered on the abysmal. Though once, enamored of pretty Catherine Lindsay, the top speller in his class, he proved he could excel. Through hard work and a bit of luck he managed to place second in the class in that subject. This earned him his coveted dream: to sit right next to her. His moment of glory however, was short-lived. At the next spelling bee, as usual, she triumphed. George, heady with his former triumph, came poorly prepared. He tried, faltered and was summarily dismissed. Ashamed and heartbroken, he went back to his accustomed place at the bottom of the class. After that, he remembered, "I never tried again." No record exists of Catherine Lindsay's reaction to either his rise or fall.

But in outside activities George displayed ingenuity, perseverance and no shyness with the opposite sex. Several times he embarked on business ventures in which girls played a major role; some are described below. None of them involved anything seriously untoward, but judging from his father's angry and often stinging reactions, they might as well have.

Once he and Andy Thompson, his best friend and the local banker's son, entered a contest to name a new kind of tomato. The winner would collect a fifty-dollar prize. Andy got seventy-five cents from his mother. Mr. Marshall, not to be outdone, contributed an equal sum. The boys ordered the seed, painted a decrepit shed in back of the Marshall place green—for this was to be a *greenhouse* crop—and contracted for a continuing supply of manure from a friend whose father owned a livery stable. They grew one huge tomato, pictured it alongside a silver dollar to show the scale, proposed a name and sent the pair to the seed company. But the matter ended there, as someone else picked the winning name.

Flushed with their success as truck farmers, Andy and George, "Flicker" as he was then known to special friends, decided to become florists as well. Their flowers were wild ones, growing in a small hollow the boys had discovered. They put them up in strawberry boxes, painted the boxes with a green stripe and sold them to the very girls who earlier had bought their tomatoes. All went well—until the source of the flowers was discovered. The girls, feeling cheated by being asked to pay for flowers grown by nature alone, refused to buy any more and complained to their mothers, who informed Mr. Marshall of the scheme. The result was the sudden bankruptcy of the enterprise, and another tanning for George's backside.

Andy and George later decided to go into the maritime transport business. With the aid of a friend's father, they built a flat-bottomed boat with a large cork as a sea-cock. The craft was pressed into service as the Coal Lick Creek Ferry, Coal Lick Creek being a narrow, shallow stream crossing the Marshall's property. Their main customers were again the local girls, who discovered the ferry made a handy shortcut to school. Andy was the captain and George the purser, in charge of collecting fares.

One day the girls, halfway in the crossing, refused to pay. When George protested, they repeated their refusal, and feeling triumphant, for good measure made fun of his poor grades. Enraged, the boy pulled the cork out and amid the shrieks of his passengers, scuttled the vessel in the shallow water. Wet, and angry, the girls were forced to wade their muddy way ashore. Irate mothers were quick to inform Mr. Marshall of the event—and once again young George had to submit to his punishment.

Life for George was further complicated by having an older brother who was openly favored by his father, and by a sister who did extremely well at school. Stuart was six years his senior, and Margaret five, so at least during childhood, there was little George would have in common with them. Even at this early stage, however, Stuart seemed to go out of his way to distance himself from his brother. Margaret, on the other hand, did not, which did not keep George from putting frogs in her bed nor from bombing her beaux with sacks filled with water when she incurred his displeasure.

His father would talk often, long and proudly of the Marshall ancestors, of John Marshall, first chief justice of the United States, and of Colonel Thomas Marshall, father of the chief justice, who moved from Virginia's Westmoreland County to that part of Virginia then known as Kentucky, not yet a separate state. He would speak of the family home in Washington, Kentucky, of George's grandfather, six times elected to that state's legislature.

Much of this family history was seemingly of little interest to George Junior, but it left a lasting mark. Even though born in Yankee territory, throughout his life the general would think of himself as a southerner and a Virginian.

Although the family history and intellectual discourse may not have always been of interest to George, fishing and hunting trips were much welcomed. It was during these trips that George Senior sometimes allowed himself to unbend and show his small son a father's attention and concern. Marshall Senior taught his son to use a shotgun. Together they stalked and killed game, and together they dressed, cooked and ate their kill.

Once, on a fishing expedition along the Youghiogheny River, George and his father were separated from two grown-up companions. The two friends of his father decided to try their luck in a renowned upstream spot, one too far off for the little boy's short legs. Left behind, the Marshalls climbed over some rocks, and found a pool. After some judicious study, George declared it to be a good one. Dubious but willing, Mr. Marshall gave George—who in his opinion was still too small to handle a reel—a pole with a string and two hooks baited with minnows. The elder Marshall moved a little further upstream. As luck would have it, the boy almost at once caught two good-sized bass. That seemed to set the tempo for both father and son. By the end of the day, their creels overflowing, they counted over 30 fish. That evening on returning to camp, they found the other two fishermen sitting, long-faced and empty-handed. Throughout his life, the general fondly recalled with what shared pride and camaraderie he and his father had showed off their catch to family and friends.

In his mother George found both a doting friend and a buffer between him and his authoritarian father. A tall, stately woman, Laura Bradford Marshall kept him well supplied with cookies, love and understanding. To her he could confide his fears, misadventures and hopes. She was often willing to overlook his shortcomings, and in her he found the encouragement needed to pursue his objectives without fear of criticism or reproach. More than once she not only protected him from the results of his antics, but actually laughed and enjoyed them. In later years he would fondly tell of one incident in particular.

It all started innoncently enough when George and Andy decided to raise little bantam roosters. The cocky banties like to fight. That made the boys curious, so they decided to raise bigger Georgia Reds. These full-sized birds were often used in cockfighting, an illegal activity in Pennsylvania. In the cockpit, as the fighting arena is known, two birds were squared off against each other. The loser usually was killed or maimed in the fight—with cheering spectators gambling on the outcome.

When their birds were full grown, the boys could not resist the temptation to pit them against others, so they asked an older friend to enter their cocks in one of the many underground cockfights. One time, eager to see how their birds were performing, they sneaked into the fight. Not long after their arrival the local sheriff raided the cockpit, but in the ensuing confusion, the boys managed to scamper out undetected. Very much afraid that the police, aware they had not caught all the men, would still be lurking about, the boys separated and hid in the woods. As darkness settled, George, deciding that the coast might by now be clear, began to creep out of the forest. Before long he realized that someone else was out there too, for he could hear the occasional controlled rustle of a body moving through the trees, following his nearly every move. For an hour or so, Marshall remembered, "I scouted him, and he scouted me." Finally, and much to his relief, he discovered that the menacing presence that had been shadowing him was Andy. "We were the only people there."

This, however, solved only half the problem. By now it was well past midnight, and reentering home undetected wouldn't be easy. After the boys reached town and again separated, George stealthily climbed up to his quarters. No sooner had he gotten in bed than his mother quietly came into his room. George confessed the whole story. "Parts of it she thought were very funny, and I remember she laughed until she cried." No lecture or harsh words came from her, but at the end it was clear to both that he "was not going back to any other chicken fight and go through that again."

When the time came for George's entry into college, there was no doubt that he wanted to follow a military career. But West Point was out of the question for political as well as academic reasons, since appointments were made by Republican members of Congress and his father was a prominent Democrat. And of course there was George's abysmal school record.

The alternative was Virginia Military Institute. Stuart, his older brother, had graduated from there, as had several other Marhalls. Colonel Charles Marshall, a cousin and former aide-de-camp to General Robert E. Lee, wrote to General Scott Shipp, the superintendent, recommending George. To nearly everybody's relief, the boy was admitted.

His record of minimal school effort might have continued at VMI, but for his overhearing Stuart telling their mother that George ought to be kept from going, because in all likelihood he would disgrace the Marshall name. The impact of these words raised him from his scholastic lethargy and, as the general would later say, "That made more impression on me than all the instructors, parental pressure or anything else. I decided then and there that I was going to wipe Stuart's eye."

To finance his schooling, Mrs. Marshall sold some property in Augusta, Kentucky, and in September 1897 George was finally sent off—a week late, thanks to an outbreak of typhoid fever which felled him as well.

Arriving at Lexington, Virginia, still a convalescent, the lanky 16-year-old boy was greeted by a bugle call sounding assembly. He watched as the battalion under the orders of its cadet officers fell in. Impressed by their precision, and proud that he would soon be one of them, George wrote his father that he was not homesick and that he was going to like it.

VMI academic standards might have been lax, but under General Scott Shipp, military duties and traditions were taken most seriously. General Thomas J. "Stonewall" Jackson was the institute's patron saint. Jackson had gone from teaching there to his meteoric career in the Confederate army. After Jackson died of complications resulting from his having been wounded at the battle of Chancellorsville in 1863, he was brought to VMI to lie in state in his old classroom and was buried in the Lexington Cemetery.

The most solemn day at VMI is the commemoration of the battle of New Market on May 15, 1864, when all 225 cadets, some as young as 15 years old, were pressed into combat. Ten died charging the Union line. Forty-seven others were wounded, as was their commander, then Colonel Shipp. Nearly a month later, under General Hunter, advancing Union troops shelled and set fire to the VMI campus. Adjoining VMI is Washington and Lee University, where the most revered figure of the South, General Robert E. Lee, would end his days as president. VMI under Shipp strove to keep the ideals and traditions of the Confederacy very much alive.

Life at the institute was spartan. "Growlie," a concoction of unknown origin whose effect on the digestive system was not always agreeable, was too often the fare, giving the term "mess" an unintentioned meaning. (In military language, mess refers to meals, as in mess hall or mess time.) Living accommodations were not much better. The barracks that survived Hunter's torch bore and still bear the marks of cannon shot. The place was poorly heated, and Virginia winters can be quite cold.

At VMI freshmen were known as "rats" and were not treated much better than their namesakes by upperclassmen. Freshmen were forced to sleep with their windows open. Many a winter morning saw the "rats" shaking snow from their blankets before morning assembly. George was soon put to the test. In his case it was squatting over a bayonet for as long as he could. Willpower exceeded strength, and as a result George was wounded in the buttock. Such hazing was strictly forbidden, but accepting the spirit of the trial, Marshall did not reveal the true cause of his wound—and won the acceptance of his schoolmates.

There was a fit between VMI and George. The soldierly qualities that General Shipp valued most—discipline, endurance and command—were the ones on which Marshall began to thrive. Academically he was still a mediocre student. Nevertheless, at the end of his first year, he headed the class list as First Corporal. His second year was uneventful. He ended it once again heading the list, now as First Sergeant.

Going home to Uniontown in the summer of 1899, he witnessed the return from the Philippines of Company C of the Tenth Pennsylvania Regiment. The Spanish-American War having been won, the United States had almost unwittingly become a colonial power. These troops were but the vanguard of Americans who would be fighting against Philippine independence. Blissfully unaware of the contradiction to American ideals these troops represented, Uniontown turned out in full force to welcome them home. Their reception by the town was triumphal. Within three years Marshall was to see firsthand the place from which they had returned.

September arrived, and Marshall selected the civil engineering path at VMI. At the end of the year, his scholastic ranking remained in the middle of his class. But his leadership qualities, and the respect he had won within the cadet corps, were reflected in two honors. At the Final Ball, First Sergeant Marshall was to lead the Ring Figure with his dance partner. For this his mother was invited as a chaperone. And he was to fulfill his dream at VMI by being unanimously chosen as next year's first captain, or the new cadet leader of the corps.

By now George Catlett Marshall was a filled-out, ramrod-straight six-footer. Not only did he have the physical appearance of a soldier, but his demeanor already exuded the aura of command that would be his for a lifetime. His confidence as a soldier was obvious—but he was to remain a mediocre scholar to the end of his VMI days.

As his senior year passed, Marshall became more aloof and austere. He had already discovered that distance was one price of command authority, and he was willing to pay it. He had few intimate friends beside his roommates, Nick Nicholson and Philip Peyton. As cadet first captain, his rank and duties separated him from the mass of the corps. At mess times, his table was shared only by the three members of his staff.

But life had a big surprise for the young soldier. She was called Lily, though her proper name was Elizabeth Carter Coles. By all accounts she was an auburn-haired beauty and heiress to some of Virginia's most distinguished names, if not fortunes. Twenty-six to Marshall's twenty, she had been the belle of VMI for several years. George's older brother Stuart, among others, had been an aspirant for her hand. Marshall had seen her before; her pony and trap were a familiar sight in and around the VMI grounds.

Lily lived with her mother in her grandfather's house, hard by the Limit Gates of the Institute. One day Marshall, strolling by, heard her playing the piano. She played so well, that entranced, he stopped to listen. Later he declared her "the finest amateur pianist I have ever heard." Though he could shout commands clear across the parade ground, he could not find the voice or the courage to speak to her. After listening for a while, he left. He was to return with reinforcements for several more discreet and distant musical evenings. Eventually, he was noticed, the door was opened and our reticent admirer was finally let in.

It was love at first sight. The dour, stern first captain was so smitten that he openly courted her. Not satisfied with the time regulations allowed for social activities, he took to seeing her

An austere-looking George Marshall as a cadet at Virginia Military Institute (George C. Marshall Research Library)

after evening formation. This was a willful violation of VMI rules—and no small matter, particularly for the first captain whose example should inspire the corps. Given General Shipp's strict view of rules, his evening forays were apt to cost him rank, even expulsion—and with that his dream of an army career. But he was neither discovered nor reported. Later he stated the obvious—"I was much in love"—an understatement if there ever was one.

The feeling was reciprocated. Miss Lily, the flirt of Lexington, had been smitten too. It has been said that after first seeing the first captain she declared, "I intend to marry him." In any event, what time either had was spent with the other; and marriage was very much on their minds.

There was one problem though. Were this West Point, Marshall upon graduation would be assured of a second lieutenant's commission—and the attendant income. VMI did not offer such a guarantee. A means of obtaining a commission needed to be found.

Marshall was lucky. Because of the Philippine insurrection against the U.S. occupation, the army would be commissioning 1,200 new second lieutenants. The catch was that in the highly politicized climate of the times, these appointments were viewed as plums to be distributed among the party faithful. Nomination for the post must have first been obtained. Only then would a test follow to determine the eligibility of each candidate.

For this, his father's help was enlisted. The elder Marshall first wrote to Shipp asking for his evaluation of George's military future. The general answered, "He is as well qualified for an officer of infantry as any man who has ever been turned out here." He added that "he could with complete confidence state that if commissioned in the Army, young Marshall will in all respects soon take his stand much above the average West Point graduate." Assured that his son was indeed topnotch military material, Marshall Senior pulled out all the stops. His not inconsiderable political clout was brought into full play. One of his principal intermediaries was John S. Wise, a graduate of VMI, indeed one of the cadets who fought in the Battle of New Market. In addition, Wise had ready access to President William McKinley, as one of the organizers of his presidential campaign.

He sent a personal note to McKinley. "This boy's kinsman, the illustrious John Marshall, was a captain in the 11th Virginia commanded by my great-grandfather during the Revolution . . . , a name this boy bears most worthily—I heartily commend him."

George, however, was not ready to rely upon letters alone. Assuming the kind of initiative that again and again would help him achieve his goals, he took himself to Washington. Once there—uninvited—he showed up at the White House.

> I had no appointment of any kind. The office was on the second floor. I think the President's bedroom, as I knew it in Mr. [Franklin] Roosevelt's day, must have been Mr. McKinley's office. The old colored man [the head usher] asked me if I had an appointment and I told him I didn't. He said I would never get in, that there wasn't any possibility. I sat there and watched people, some ten or fifteen, go in by appointment, stay ten minutes, and be excused. Finally a man and his daughter went in with this old colored man escorting them. I attached myself to the tail of the procession and gained the President's office. The old colored man frowned at me on his way out but I stood pat. After the people had met the President they also went out, leaving me standing there. Mr. McKinley in a very nice manner asked what I wanted, and I stated my case. I don't recall what he said, but from that I think flowed my appointment or rather my authority to appear for examination.

Whether thanks to his own audacity—or to his father's efforts—Marshall got his chance to take the examination. His average was 84.8, one of the highest marks among the applicants. He scored 100 in Physique and in Moral Character and Antecedents. He received an 89 in History and a 75 in English—everything else was downhill from there. His lowest score was a 42 in International Law.

On February 2, 1902, Marshall finally received his much-longed-for second lieutenant's commission. He was immediately ordered to report to Fort Myer, Virginia, 10 days later, for duty in the Philippines.

Lily now told him that in spite of her fresh and vibrant demeanor she was in fact a semi-invalid. Her heart had a defective valve, a condition known as a mitral insufficiency, so she could not have children or undergo excessive excitement. As he already knew, even dancing was too much for her.

Undeterred, Marshall insisted on the wedding. So on February 11, 1902, only days after his commission, Lily and he were married. The hastily arranged ceremony took place at the Coles home in Lexington. The wedding party was small: George's parents, brother and sister, a few Coles relatives and a handful of friends. The next day the newlyweds left for Washington, D.C., for an anticipated one-day honeymoon in that city's fanciest new hotel, the New Willard. After that Lily was to return to Lexington and her mother's. The young couple's separation was expected to last the two years of George's tour of duty.

George C. Marshall was now 21, married and an officer in the army of the United States. His dreams had begun to be realized.

2

A SPECIAL OFFICER

On April 12, 1902, newly minted Second Lieutenant George C. Marshall began his military career in earnest as he boarded the old army transport *Kilpatrick* in San Francisco. His destination: 7,000 miles away in Mindoro, the Philippine Islands, America's new possessions freshly wrested from Spain.

The United States entered into war with Spain in 1898, two years after Emilio Aguinaldo and his Insurrectos had risen against Madrid, and a year after the islands had declared their independence. The Filipinos originally saw U.S. intervention as a help to their cause—certainly not as an effort to impose another foreign government on them. Soon though, they were disabused of their original view, when American troops, arriving in substantial numbers, came to take control of the country. Poorly armed, divided among themselves and weakened by their defeats at the hands of the Spaniards, the Filipinos were no match for the new invaders. Nevertheless, while unable to put organized formations on the field, they were quite capable of waging guerrilla warfare, and did so with varying degrees of success.

It was to counteract guerrilla activities that Marshall and his newly commissioned brethren had been recruited and sent to the islands. Further, in order to mollify Filipino sensitivities, control was taken away from General Arthur MacArthur, celebrated in the United States as "the Conqueror of the Philippines." (General MacArthur was the father of young Douglas MacArthur, also destined to become a famous general.) William Howard Taft, a civilian, took over as governor of the islands. He was later to become president of the United

States. However meaningful this move might have appeared stateside, it failed to impress the Filipino guerrillas.

On arrival at Mindoro in May 1902, Marshall reported to headquarters, Thirtieth Infantry Regiment. Mindoro was and is hardly the South Pacific island of one's dreams. It is covered with steaming jungles and forbidding mountains, and at that time was home to bands of armed bandits, called "Ladrones," as well as guerrillas. Garrison duty was stiffling and boring—made worse by an unstable commander and unruly troops. Then cholera, a disease that dehydrates the body and often results in death, struck. Brought in by fishermen running the Manila quarantine where the epidemic had begun, it decimated the local native population. By allowing only boiled water to be drunk and by strict enforcement of sanitation, American soldiers were spared. However, they buried Filipinos by the hundreds, as our young lieutenant remembered:

> The first time . . . I found the soldiers peacefully eating their supper on a pile of new coffins. Later on, there weren't any coffins. The deaths came too rapidly and they were buried by the dozens in a trench. . . . The sides of the [hospital] tents were rolled up so you could see the patients on the gold metal cots without any sheets, their legs drawn up almost under their chins, generally shrieking from the agony of convulsions. But they didn't last long . . . I don't remember anybody recovering at that time.

Mercifully the epidemic was over by the end of June. Marshall was then ordered to join a detachment in Mangarin, a small outpost. There he would be the only officer. The toughened troopers of this unit viewed him as green and mild-mannered, and like soldiers everywhere, waited for a chance to test his mettle. It arrived soon enough. Out on patrol in search of bandits and guerrillas, they came upon a small horse surrounded by natives. The large gash on its side was the result of a crocodile bite. Not far beyond was a small stream wide and deep enough to be home to crocodiles, but still shallow enough to be forded. With Marshall at the lead, the men entered the water, their rifles held high. Nearing the other side, the shout suddenly went up, "Crocodile," and the soldiers scrambled forward, "accidentally" trampling their lieutenant into the water and mud.

Lieutenant Marshall (center, bottom row) with fellow soliders of the Thirtieth Infantry in the Philippines, 1902 (George C. Marshall Research Library)

Without saying a word, Marshall had the detachment fall in and shoulder arms, and led them again across the stream. Upon the last man reaching the other shore, he barked, "To the rear, march!" and the men once more slogged through the dark muddy water. He halted them, held a rifle inspection and fell them out of formation. Nothing was said of the event by either the green officer or the seasoned soldiers. There was no need. The troopers had taken the new lieutenant's measure, and he had measured up.

For a year and a half, Marshall would be stationed in the Philippines. He would see service in the capital, Manila, as well as in the distant, isolated outposts where the guerrillas were active. In the long hours of garrison duty, he would study the Insurrection, the cruelties committed by the Americans as well as by the Filipinos and the reprisals each exacted from the other. In so doing he would learn to appreciate both points of view. His duties would even include a brief stint of guard duty at Malahi Island, a military prison.

In October 1904, replacements arrived. His comment was terse and to the point: "Their depression when they saw the place was great. Our elation when we left was even greater."

For years the high command of the U.S. Army in Washington had been trying to upgrade the service—which was viewed by the civilian government as hardly more than a glorified national police force. To achieve professional status, its officers needed further military education. To that end the closed Infantry and Cavalry School in Fort Leavenworth, Kansas, was reopened as the Army School of the Line for a one-year course. The top students would then go on to a two-year stint at the Army Staff College. The intent was to model the resulting upper army echelons after the European concept of a General Staff, a body trained to organize and direct large troop formations. Obviously the officers successfully completing the courses were destined for high-ranking positions.

Second Lieutenant Marshall was selected to attend. A few weeks after his admittance, the army ordered that no one below the rank of captain was to be enrolled, but he and three other lieutenants managed to circumvent the new ruling.

Marshall arrived at Fort Leavenworth in August 1906, after serving for nearly three years in Oklahoma and Texas outposts. Long-suffering Lily remained in Virginia. Since their marriage, they had spent more time apart than together. He again took bachelor quarters. There would be 54 students in his class, all older than he, and with much greater experience. He was also fully aware that here academic work—his old nemesis—would really count. If he was to succeed he would have to learn to study. With characteristic perseverance and tenacity, he did. Of this he was later to say, "I finally got into the habit of study which I never really had before . . . I became pretty automatic at the business . . . [but] it was the hardest work I ever did in my life."

It *was* hard work. Because Marshall had problems sleeping and in an effort to stay awake and concentrate at night, he constantly shined his boots. The effort paid off. To those who figured he would not even make the top half, he gave the lie. Not only was he within what would be the quota for the second year, but he finished among the top five of his class. And no one had more dazzling boots.

Christmas 1906 and New Year's would find Marshall taking his exams for his promotion to first lieutenant. To no one's surprise, he made the grade, and was promoted in March 1907. He had then been a soldier for five years and he was 26 years old. Lily at last was able to join him and moved to Leavenworth.

Teaching at Leavenworth was Major John F. Morrison, an exceptionally gifted instructor and military thinker, an officer who would leave a deep imprint upon a whole army generation. Unlike most of his contemporaries on the faculty, he was able to recognize a military principle *and* put it into action. Marshall remembered him admiringly:

> His problems were short and always contained a "knock-out" if you failed to recognize the principle involved in meeting the situation. Simplicity and dispersion became fixed qualities in my mind never to be forgotten . . . He spoke a tactical language I had never heard from any other officer. He was self-educated, reading constantly, and creating and solving problems for himself. He taught me all I have ever known of tactics.

In the meantime, the school year came to an end in January 1908 and thanks to persistence and an innate sense of soldiering, Marshall found himself at the head of his class, his place assured in the Staff College.

A request came soon thereafter from the Pennsylvania National Guard for instructors from the army. Five were selected, Marshall among them. Unlike the regular army, the National Guard could muster large formations—even if only for a few days each summer. The Pennsylvania assignment gave Marshall his first chance at commanding a substantial body of troops and at dealing with the "citizen-soldier," another novel experience. He was so successful with the militia that at the end of the summer, he was asked to return the following year.

Come autumn 1908 Marshall was back at Fort Leavenworth. That year the French and German General Staffs, two of the world's most respected, were studied. The Civil War was refought with student groups acting as chief of staff to various generals, including Robert E. Lee. The 1904–05 Russo-Japanese War, which startled the world because of the quick Russian defeat and which turned Japan into a major power, was deeply probed—its results made even more immediate by Major Morrison's own direct and disquieting observations. Morrison had been alongside Japanese formations while they trounced the Russians. He was much impressed with their fighting ability and spirit. The victorious Japanese and their tactics would remain of great interest to Marshall, and be of much value in his schooling.

The basic duty of a general staff officer is to generate "what-if" scenarios to various courses of action—before such action takes place. Part of that is the assembly and supply of the elements that will be required, from shoes and blankets, to guns, troops and ambulances—as well as the roads and means to get all these to and from the front. Once a choice is made, the staff officer will weigh the resulting alternatives and present them to the field commander with his recommendations and rationale. To be successful, he must always stay one jump ahead of events in that most complex and unpredictable of human endeavors, warfare.

Obviously such a position requires a rare combination of military talent, diplomacy, flexibility of thinking, physical stamina, understanding of human nature—and large doses of just plain luck. Few men can claim to possess most—let alone all—of these virtues. George Marshall was one of those few. At the end of his second year at the Army Staff College, he was asked to remain as an instructor. Marshall was to teach military art (the conduct of warfare) and engineering.

In the summer of 1909, George Marshall visited his family. It would be the last time he saw his father alive. Mr. Marshall would die that September of a heart attack. He would leave an estate to his wife and children amounting to $26,000, a tidy sum for the times. The children assigned their shares to their mother. This, together with some property of her own, would make her self-sufficient for the rest of her life.

Back in Leavenworth, the Staff College soon discovered what the Pennsylvania militia already knew: Marshall was a born teacher. He took to his classes with enthusiasm and tact. The latter was much needed, since his students all outranked him, and a fair number were suspicious of his newfangled ways. Then there were those for whom seniority was paramount. This group would have been more than pleased if Marshall had failed, for they deeply resented what they viewed as his unearned position. Marshall did well, but he also knew that by army regulations, he must return to a field posting and garrison duty at the end of the term.

However, Marshall had accumulated four months of leave. After wrangling an additional month's extension at half pay, and armed with his savings, he and Lily headed for Europe in a cattle boat carrying six passengers as well as hundreds of mooing cows. If it was not the Grand Tour, it certainly managed to include some of the Continent's highlights. In Paris, they finagled a forbidden lunch at Versailles, home to the former French kings; in Rome they talked their way into the palace of the king of Italy; in England, they watched the maneuvers of the British army. They visited Austria and spent three weeks in Florence. On their way back, the couple stopped in Trieste, and squeezed another layover in Algiers before crossing the Atlantic and landing happy and exhausted in New York.

Marshall's new assignment was as commandant, Company D, 24th Infantry, hard by Watertown, in upstate New York. He arrived in the middle of a bitterly cold winter, but his stay there was not to be long.

The new chief of staff of the army, General Leonard Wood, was bent on organizing his service into a force capable of fighting major engagements. The regular army was scattered across the nation in small garrisons designed for the needs of the Indian wars of the previous century. They no longer served any military purpose. General Wood, following in his predecessor's footsteps, attempted to consolidate these garrisons, but failed. Then as now, the local army payroll was considered political spoils, and no congressman was going to allow *that* pork barrel to leave his district without a major fight.

The result was that the U.S. Army's largest effective combat unit was the batallion—a mere 700 men or so. Further, the army itself was its own worse enemy. In years past it had set up a system of bureaus—each of which acted more or less independently—and each of which, fearful of losing its prerogatives, obstructed any move to centralize command. Wood attempted to change this as well, but here too, he failed, and for the same reason: politics. In the meantime, events on the Mexican frontier began to show the wisdom of Wood's thinking.

By 1910 the Mexican Revolution was well on its way, and it was obvious that the United States could not stand aloof and uninvolved, since its interests were affected. The leader of the revolution, Francisco Madero, urged his followers on from Texas. U.S. involvement would later include diplomatic efforts and then military force in efforts to dislodge President Huerta.

In an attempted show of strength, the army tried to concentrate a division in San Antonio, Texas. Since no such unit existed even on paper, it was designated the Maneuver Division. Marshall was assigned to it in March 1911.

His duty was with the signal corps. Using the techniques he had learned and taught at the Staff College, Marshall went through the exercise of mobilizing troops and creating a command and communications center. Troop movements were simulated simply by sending messages whose acknowledgment signaled completion of the specific action. Three planes and several radios, including three airborne ones, were put at Marshall's disposal. The planes represented a pair of advancing infantry columns and a cavalry brigade. Once the aircraft were aloft, the cavalry pilot radioed what could well be the first use of this wireless transmission in American maneuvers. The transmission read, "I am west of the manure pile"—a phrase that might have aptly described the readiness of the U.S. Army as well. Ninety days later, American troops were still arriving. Neither the Mexicans nor the foreign military observers were impressed.

In August 1913 Marshall was again posted to the Philippines, now as a company commander. The problem was no longer the Insurrectos, the Filipino guerrillas Marshall had once gone after, but the phenomenal growth in power and ambition of Imperial Japan. Within about two decades, in a series of brilliant and ruthless actions, the Japanese had defeated China and Russia, conquered Manchuria and annexed Korea. It did not take a military genius to see that the Philippines might be an inviting next target. San Francisco and reinforcements were over 7,000 miles to the east, while Formosa, then already under Japanese control for close to 20 years, lay a mere 300 miles away, about a day's journey for a steamship of the time. And U.S.–Japan relations had cooled to a frosty level, thanks to anti-Japanese legislation in California and restrictive U.S. immigration quotas.

Nervous about these developments, the American army bolstered its meager defenses on the Philippine Islands. It also wanted to test the adequacy of those forces. Marshall was given the post of adjutant to the "White Force," which was to invade Luzon. The "Brown Force" would act as defenders. The exact date was kept secret, but it was known that it would be during January. On January 22 the "White Force" was given its orders: concentrate its forces in Batangas Bay within three days and then attack Manila.

The "White Force" was led by an aging colonel overly fond of his flask. After a few blunders, an upset commanding general proposed to relieve him. Instead, at Marshall's urging, the old colonel was left in command but instructed not to interfere with his adjutant's actions. But then the "White Force" chief of staff became ill and had to be hospitalized. This left Marshall as the only one with full knowledge of the plan of action. A mere lieutenant was thus to direct the actions of the bulk of the U.S. forces in the Philippines.

The exercise was deemed a success—and the myth of Marshall was born. Two men, later to become generals in their own right, contributed the most. Lieutenant Henry (Hap) Arnold, who led the Army Air Force during World War II, wrote to his wife, "I have seen a future Chief of Staff in action." And Colonel Hagood offered even more extravagant praise in comparing Marshall to the South's revered General Stonewall Jackson.

In Europe, meantime, August 1914 saw the outbreak of World War I. On one side were the Entente Cordiale powers—France, Great Britain, Belgium, Portugal, Russia and Italy. On the other were principally the German and Austro-Hungarian empires. Other nations would in time join the fray. On the Western Front, German troops invaded Belgium and France, on the Eastern Front Austrian forces sought to subdue Serbian nationalists, and the Russians attacked Germany's East Prussia.

The Japanese, allied to the French and British, wasted no time in consolidating and extending the positions they already held in mainland China. Their actions could not but increase the potential threat to the American forces in the Philippines. A new exercise designed by Marshall for U.S. troops showed that a Japanese invasion via Lingayen Gulf would be successful. Some 25 years later during World War II, history would prove Marshall's assessment correct.

While pleased with the results of his work, Marshall looked at his age and rank and was disheartened. He was pushing 35, and was still only a lieutenant. It did not matter to him that he was well regarded and had by his efforts already won the notice of powerful generals. The peacetime army was driven by seniority, and there were far too many older lieutenants awaiting promotion ahead of him. The army, perhaps aware of his unhappiness and unwilling to lose him, ordered him stateside to appear before a promotion board. Because of his service at Leavenworth, the requisite examination was waived. In October 1916, Lieutenant Marshall became Captain Marshall.

President Woodrow Wilson, with the twin specters of World War I and the Mexican situation, realized the need for a stronger, larger army and created the Officer Reserve Corps. Marshall's new assignment was to train the volunteers for the new corps. The first camp was at Monterey, just outside San Francisco. Since the prospective officers received no pay and were expected to cover their own expenses as well, it was not surprising that they thought it should be a pleasant and comfortable experience. The call to arms was taken up by the fashionable crowd—about the only ones who could afford the time and money involved.

Marshall had already had experience with this type of crew before, in his days with the Pennsylvania National Guard, so he knew how to handle them. So deftly did he do so that they dubbed him "Dynamite" Marshall. From California he went to Utah for a similar tour. While there he received in his efficiency report just about the highest praise another officer can give. To the question, "would you like to have him under your command?" Colonel Hagood wrote "yes" and added, "but I would prefer to serve under his command." Hagood went on to recommend that he be made a brigadier general: "He is of the proper age, has had the training and experience and possesses the ability to command large bodies of troops in the field." The proposal was not as far afield as one might think. After all, only a few years earlier Captain Pershing overnight had become Brigadier General Pershing at the stroke of the president's pen.

By 1914 the Mexican Revolution had spilled into the United States, where the reformist Francisco Madero rallied support for his cause. Later, Pancho Villa and his men, in an effort to involve the United States in their quarrel with the Mexican central government, happily raided U.S. border towns with guns blazing. At first the United States stood helplessly by, its southern frontier undefended. Soon though, army units were dispatched to Texas, Arizona and New Mexico. Villa's attacks were widely dispersed, and garrisoning every border settlement was out of the question. The alternative was to threaten to strike back, and if that failed, to fight the attackers on their own territory. Eventually, in 1916, Brigadier General Jack Pershing wound up leading an expedition of 12,000 men deep into Mexico in a fruitless search for Villa. Marshall had unsuccessfully sought a slot in Pershing's force.

While there was little dissent about the Mexican war, the United States was deeply divided about the ongoing European conflict. This was partly due to the strong ethnic ties of the vast population of recent European immigrants to this country. There was also a widely held view of Great Britain as "perfidious Albion"—"perfidious" meaning treacherous and Albion being the ancient and literary name for Britain. This was a legacy of previous British-American wars. Other causes of anti-British sentiment were the feeling of the Irish toward their former masters, and that the well-known axiom "divide and conquer" had for long been England's path to supremacy.

Soon though, Britain's huge purchases of foodstuffs and armaments from the United States, coupled with effective propaganda and the incredible blunders by the Germans, pushed U.S. public opinion toward the Allies. Perhaps the most important element was the introduction by the Germans of a new naval weapon, the U-boat. Not only was the deadly effectiveness of the submarine frightening, but it also appeared to violate the accepted concepts of warfare. Its use was viewed as sneaky and treacherous. Then on May 7, 1915, came the sinking of the *Lusitania*, a British passenger ship secretly carrying armaments. Torpedoed without warning off the coast of Ireland, she took nearly 1,200 people to the bottom, including 128 Americans. That was viewed by President Woodrow Wilson as the last straw. Amid strong opposition, Wilson declared war on Germany on April 6, 1917.

Declaring war is one thing. Engaging in it is quite another. To be successful in such an endeavor, a good army is necessary.

And for practical purposes, given the scale of action in Europe, America did not have one. When President Wilson decided to send General Pershing and a division abroad, there was not a single division in the American army to be had. Pershing would be in France to show the flag and ostensibly to set up a base for the incoming American soldiers. In reality the move was made to gain time.

Four regiments were selected to form the new division, but being understrength themselves, their rosters were filled by men from other units. Since a divisional headquarters did not exist, one was created out of officers looted from other formations. Untrained, disorganized and mostly armed only with rifles, they would be shipped out as the First Infantry Division almost two months after Pershing's departure. The effort so exhausted the army's resources that it would be four months before the Second Division, in similar condition, could be shipped out. After that, the problems would be sorted out, and the next units to arrive in France would be, if not battle-ready, at least recognizable as military formations.

In the meantime Marshall, eager for combat duty, tried to get himself attached to the Pershing staff. Unsuccessful there, after much effort he managed to get himself posted to the First Division as assistant chief of staff to General William L. Sibert, its commanding officer. Sibert, under whom Marshall had served before, was well pleased to have him aboard. At last an overaged Captain George Marshall was to see combat duty. But this duty would not be as he had hoped; it would not lead to the line command he so coveted.

3

WORLD WAR I—THE PERSHING INFLUENCE

Marshall's career as a General Staff officer was to crystallize with World War I and his relationship with General John "Blackjack" Pershing. Pershing was the commander of the American Expeditionary Force (AEF), as the U.S. troops sent to Europe were called. It would be in the battlefields of France that Marshall would be introduced to truly larger military concepts; and it would be at Pershing's side that he would become familiar with power in the highest circles.

A 36-year-old Captain George C. Marshall and the forward elements of the First Infantry Division landed in France on June 26, 1917. Marshall was the first man to come ashore after General Sibert. The division was the spearhead of the 2-million man AEF that the United States was committing to France. Here at last were fresh new soldiers who had come to turn the tide.

What the French did not know was that the First Division was little more than a uniformed rabble, for most of its men were raw recruits with great enthusiasm but little military skill. Turning these men into soldiers would be Pershing's first monumental task, one that would require time and seasoned officers—both in very short supply in the U.S. Army. The French were therefore stunned and angered when they saw month after month pass, and no Americans appeared in the front lines.

The inability to commit the as yet untrained American soldiers to the trenches put Pershing under extreme pressure. The Allies hungered for the American reinforcements; the public at home clamored for U.S. victories; and the men themselves were tired of endless drills and chafed at the bit as they felt the envy and contempt of the combat-hardened French and British soldiers in their sector.

It was during this period that Pershing announced on short notice an inspection visit of First Division Headquarters. Already dissatisfied with General Sibert's performance, he asked to see an exercise that would demonstrate the status of combat-readiness of the unit. To that end, Marshall, as acting chief of staff and in the absence of General Sibert and the not-yet-landed divisional chief of staff, set up the exercise as prescribed by Pershing's own headquarters.

Pershing arrived, and almost simultaneously, so did General Sibert and his fresh-from-the-States chief of staff. The exercise completed, Sibert, who because of his absence had no prior knowledge of the maneuver, was asked by Pershing for his comments. His response was obviously not satisfactory, for Pershing then testily turned to the hapless divisional chief of staff. When the poor man did no better than Sibert, the short-tempered commander in chief burst into a long tirade berating all present, especially General Sibert, whom Marshall considered a fine officer. Stung to the quick by what he saw as a gross injustice to his superiors, Marshall—literally taking his own career in his hands—reached out and tapped the turning Pershing on the arm.

"General Pershing," he said, "there is something to be said here and I think I should say it because I have been here the longest." Pershing stopped, and staring in contempt at the audacious officer, asked in clipped tones, "What have you to say?" For what seemed an eternity, Marshall spoke and Pershing listened. Exactly what was said was not recorded, but it was clear that in Marshall's view it was the exercise itself as ordered by AEF headquarters that was at fault. When asked about it in later years, Marshall, would only grin and recall he had had "an inspired moment."

When Marshall had finished, Pershing, calmer now, said, "You must appreciate the troubles we have." Marshall not giving an inch, replied, "Yes, General, but we have them everyday too, and they have to be solved before night." At that Pershing coldly stared at him, turned on his heel and left. All present agreed—they had just witnessed the end of Marshall's promising career. But weeks went by, and the expected Pershing thunderbolt failed to materialize. Instead Pershing, in his contacts with the First Division, often sought Marshall out.

By the autumn of 1917 the situation on the Western Front had become more and more desperate, with French losses mounting steadily. As a result, American soldiers were finally deployed near the city of Nancy in an area that, since 1914, had been tranquil. But the Germans had a surprise in store.

Under cover of darkness, at 3 A.M. on November 3, German infantry swarmed over a green American unit, killing 3 men and taking 12 prisoners before returning to their own lines. But the raid, which had been intended to demonstrate the ineptness of the Americans, had a wholly unanticipated result.

To the French and the Americans, after five months of waiting, came the sudden realization that with these first casualties, the AEF was really committed to the war. At last the Americans could in truth say, "Lafayette, we are here," and know that the French now had reason to believe them.

After the initial German onslaught in 1914, which had completely overrun Belgium and invaded northern France as well, the Western Front had frozen into trench warfare some 100 to 150 miles into French territory. The front extended roughly from Lille southward to the Swiss border. Savage attacks and counterattacks had been made by both sides, bringing death to thousands, even though only a paltry few miles would be gained or lost. The last attack was the British offensive in Flanders, which had cost the Allies a quarter of a million men.

In 1917 both the Allies and the Germans saw the American entry into the war as the one element that could tip the balance and thus end the stalement; for as things stood, victory was nowhere in sight for either side. For Germany, whose industrial and agricultural base had been stretched to the limit thanks to the effectiveness of the British naval blockade, American involvement not only meant millions of fresh Allied soldiers, but also access for the British and French to food, clothing, armaments—all the things that were in short supply in Germany.

To the German High Command, there was only one answer: Deliver a single decisive blow that would either end the war or would sufficiently improve their position so they could ask for an armistice—a cease-fire—with neither side the victor.

Their chance came in the spring of 1918, with the collapse of the Russian armies as the result of the Bolshevik Revolution. Now 100 battle-tested German divisions from the Eastern Front could be shifted to France. Moving fast, they launched a major offensive on March 21.

At first they were successful, pushing the front some 50 miles deeper into France and nearly panicking the French with "Big Bertha" and their other new long-range guns that were close enough to begin shelling Paris itself. Two further offensives were to follow. Soon, however, its munitions spent and its ranks decimated, the German drive stalled. Through the summer, it seemed as though the war would continue as before.

But the autumn of 1918 was to prove different. The British and French, who until then had fought under separate and often feuding commands, finally joined together, with French Marshal Ferdinand Foch as the Allied commander in chief. Pershing too had earlier insisted that his formations were to fight only under his command. But recognizing the difficulties of warfare by committee, he also placed his troops under the French marshal.

By now, Americans were pouring into France at the rate of 250,000 a month. The Allies, with a unified command, ample supplies and already a million fresh AEF troops, could at last turn the tide. Marshall, still serving with the First Division staff, hungered for a field command. Without it, he recognized, he could never attain the rank of general. Several times he asked for a line posting, even being recommended to head a brigade, which would bring him the star of a brigadier general. But General Headquarters always turned him down as being too valuable in his staff capacity. Poor Marshall was put in an odd position: by doing his job *too* well he was denied further advancement.

A staff officer is essentially an organizer and a planner. Unlike the line officer, who has direct command of troops, the staff officer's role is advisory. In its simplest terms the line officer is responsible for winning the battle; the staff officer's objective is to win the war. His rank is often lower than those he must report about. In general, the staff officer, especially the one from General Headquarters, is not well regarded by his line comrades. He is seen as a rear-echelon soldier, one without firsthand knowledge of battle conditions.

While this description fit many, it did not apply to Marshall. One of the many factors that made him a superb staff officer was his unwillingness to accept hearsay as fact. Often, on his own initative, he would venture to the front to see it for himself. He was even cited for bravery under fire. More relevant though, was his willingness to learn, to listen to the comments and experiences of line officers, to fit orders to field conditions. Marshall was even willing to "bend the book" when circumstances warranted it, a novel concept to most regular army officers of the day. Recognizing this, Pershing ordered Marshall transferred to his own AEF headquarters staff where he was promoted regularly—from captain to temporary major, lieutenant colonel and colonel.

One of Marshall's first tasks at headquarters was a distasteful one. The assignment: investigate the leadership of a captain, who, while on patrol, had managed to walk into an ambush and get 20 of his men killed. The board of inquiry, on which Marshall was the juniormost member, delegated the report responsibility to him. Marshall, feeling that the inquiry was unjust, abruptly announced he had reached a decision. The other members, startled, asked what it was. Marshall's reply: "It is to the effect that a telegram should be sent to the 77th Division by the Chief-of-Staff of the AEF congratulating them on the offensive spirit displayed in the raid, and expressing the hope that the unfortunate result would not deter the division from undertaking further offensive actions." Much to Marshall's surprise, the other board members agreed with his conclusion and with his suggestion that the telegram from GHQ be sent immediately.

Soon Marshall faced more pressing matters, for Pershing had brought him abroad just in time for the Allied counteroffensive that would in fact end the war. It was here at AEF headquarters staff that he fully came into his own. Working with General Fox Conner, he developed the plans for the only major involvements of American troops in the war. These were the attack on the St.-Mihiel (the salient line of defense there), and the AEF's participation in the Meuse-Argonne offensive. St.-Mihiel was a purely American operation involving close to a half a million men. The target was a large German-held bulge pressing

Marshall with General John "Black Jack" Pershing during World War I
(George C. Marshall Research Library)

against the Allied lines and a potential staging area for a
German attack. Both of these engagements were to be of great
significance in Marshall's later life, for they involved the move-

ment of huge armies and materiel. The offensive would, in addition, require the coordination of troops of different languages and nationalities and the engagement of two weapons still in their infancy, the tank and the airplane. All these were concepts foreign to the U.S. Army of the time. Later they were the very things he would first teach at the Army War College, and then implement when he became chief of staff in World War II.

Foch had agreed to the attack on the St.-Mihiel line of defense on the condition that it not interfere with AEF participation in the Meuse-Argonne offensive. Pershing accepted, leaving the ticklish question of how to redeploy the troops for the second engagement to Marshall. The attack on St.-Mihiel proved even more successful than anticipated, for by the third day the area had fallen into U.S. hands. In all, the Americans took 16,000 prisoners and lost 13,000 men. At last the AEF had proved itself as an army.

Then came the execution of Marshall's second task, the transfer of 400,000 of the men who had fought at St.-Mihiel to the Meuse-Argonne front—a maneuver for which only three roads were available. Not only were there the soldiers, but 3,000 pieces of artillery, 90,000 horses and 40,000 tons of artillery shells to be moved as well. And the vehicles to be used were horse-drawn wagons and trucks slightly larger than a modern pickup. As Marshall laconically stated later, "A lot of the troops walked." And the General Staff prayed. For while the American numbers were most imposing, the quality of the troops was not. St.-Mihiel had been an easy operation essentially against second-rate garrison troops, but the forthcoming encounter would pit the Franco-American forces against some of the best units the Imperial German Army could muster.

Before dawn on September 26, 1918, 2,700 Allied guns erupted over a 40-mile front, roughly one cannon every 25 yards. Half the front was held by the American First Army, half by the French Fourth Army. The objective was to regain the rail centers at Metz, Sedan and Nancy, or at least to sever these vital railway lines. This would deprive the Germans of their ability to move the men and vast stores of materiel that had been stockpiled there. Foch felt that without these supplies, the capability of the German army to continue fighting on the Western Front would end.

At the beginning, American advances were rapid, as the lightly held German first line quickly gave way. But afterward enemy resistance stiffened considerably—by September 30, only 8 miles had been gained. Because of the scarcity of roads, incredible jams developed as American and French supply columns vied for the same road space, with ambulances, reserve units, shifting artillery and ever present munition wagons delivering 3,000 tons of shells each day—often under enemy fire.

With the offensive stalled, Pershing decided to reinforce his center, for there the advance had been the smallest and slowest. To that end he summoned Marshall to oversee the task of moving in fresh divisions and moving out the exhausted line troops. It was a task Marshall, who by then held the rank of temporary colonel, handled well.

Then came the issue of the capture of the city of Sedan, and the beginning of Marshall's lifelong struggle with then Brigadier General Douglas MacArthur, son of the conqueror of the Philippines, General Arthur MacArthur.

The surrender of Sedan in the 1870 Franco-Prussian War had been seen by France as a most humiliating defeat. In 1914, Sedan had once more fallen into German hands. The French felt its recapture by French forces was needed to restore the country's stained honor. Foch therefore had made sure that the city fell well within French Fourth Army territory.

General Pershing, however, thought differently. Issuing an order contradictory to that from the Allied Supreme Command, he directed that American forces take Sedan, but his order was unclear. Two separate divisions, the First and the Forty-second, the latter led by MacArthur, each assumed *it* was to lead the attack.

In combat, every unit is given a zone of operations within which it is to restrict its activities. Not to do so is to invite chaos—never mind the distinct possibility of having one's own troops shoot at each other. The record remains murky. The order, reluctantly countersigned by Marshall, authorized U.S. troops to disregard unit boundaries in pursuit of the enemy. Delighted, the First Division streamed through the Forty-second Division and MacArthur's formations that night without notifying him. Moreover, ostensibly mistaking him for a German officer, First Division even placed MacArthur under arrest.

As a member of the General Headquarters staff, Marshall was seen by MacArthur, a line officer, as a natural enemy. From there to assuming that Marshall had favored the First Division and had tried to cheat him of glory he felt he had earned was but a short jump. Marshall would deny this to his dying day, but MacArthur's belief was to remain a permanent sore point, one that would sour his relations with Marshall. But neither the French nor the Americans were to take Sedan that day. Ironically, the city was to remain in German hands until after the armistice.

In the meantime, the other two major sectors of the Western Front were seeing similar offensives. Soon, low on munitions and food, demoralized by the ceaseless Allied attacks and their own huge losses, entire German units began to surrender. It was obvious to all that the end of the war was near.

At 11 A.M. on the eleventh day of the eleventh month of 1918, along the entire front, buglers from both armies sounded the final cease-fire. The endless war was at last over.

Marshall was to remain in Europe for nearly another year. His first assignment was to prepare contingency plans should the Germans repudiate the armistice. Afterward he was to plan for the occupation of the German zone allocated to the Americans. He carried out both tasks with distinction. In April 1919 Pershing asked that he serve as his aide, a post he would hold for several years. With that transfer came George Catlett Marshall's entry into the world of the politically as well as militarily powerful.

Marshall was a dashing 38, a colonel in a triumphant army and at the right hand of its leader. He was now to receive the accolades of the cream of society in all of the countries that Pershing toured. He would flirt with duchesses, dance with queens and step on the toes of at least one king. What polish he might have lacked he quickly acquired. He was also to see how power works at the highest circles. The men and the views he met during this period would stand him in very good stead, for 20 years later he would face the same men or their successors either as allies or enemies.

This grand tour lasted until September 1919, when the American High Command embarked for New York. There a great victory parade was held, complete with streaming ticker tape and cheering throngs. Another hero's welcome in Washington, D.C., would have Marshall by Pershing's side, marching down Pennsylvania Avenue to the White House at the head of 25,000 veterans.

A grateful Congress granted Pershing the permanent rank of General of the Army. But for Marshall, as for most of the Regular army officers who remained in the suddenly shrunken service, coming home meant a rollback in rank. Marshall returned to his permanent rank of captain, with its much lower pay and perquisites—quite different from those of the full but temporary rank of colonel he had enjoyed in France. What held him back was not incompetence, but a national concept of the soldier as a no-longer essential member of society. America was later to pay dearly for this concept.

Soon after returning from Europe in 1919, Pershing went on a national speaking tour, his political ambitions fanned by a Republican party in search of a presidential candidate. It was during these unsuccessful efforts to seek a nomination for Pershing that Marshall learned to deal with American politics. Later, when General Pershing became army chief of staff under the new administration, the freshly promoted Major Marshall would learn, as Pershing's aide, the subtleties of handling not only Congress, but the White House as well.

It was the combination of these political and military skills, acquired early in Marshall's career, that in large measure would ensure this country's success during World War II and in the postwar years.

4

BETWEEN THE WARS—A
THIRD-RATE ARMY

Afterthe patriotic fervor of 1917–1918 and after welcoming the victorious troops of the American Expeditionary Force (AEF), America had had enough of war and foreign adventures. The country wanted no part of ravaged Europe or its people. So when President Wilson proposed his League of Nations as a forum to solve international disputes peaceably, the American public recoiled and the country withheld itself from it. Isolationism spread throughout the nation, and uniforms were an unwelcome sight. People who had earlier cheered returning troops now saw soldiers simply as a burden on the public purse. Having expended its monies and shed its blood, a postwar United States adamantly held back further support, financial or otherwise, of the military.

As before, the army at the end of the war viewed itself as the nucleus around which a citizen force would be formed in the event of a national emergency. As Pershing and Marshall already foresaw it, the next war would be one in which speed and flexibility would be paramount—already, the battlefield introduction of the airplane and motorized vehicles including the tank had given ample evidence of that. To the soldiers who understood war and were prepared for it, success would come as the Germans were to prove in the early years of World War II, and the Allies later.

Nonetheless, in the 1920s Congress and the nation turned a blind eye to military needs and refused to open the national purse. The army was allowed to increase its authorized size, but without the funding to do so, its new strength could exist on paper only. Stagnation became the service's natural condition.

In Pershing, his mentor and friend, Marshall had found the kind of familial bond that he craved. The newly promoted lieutenant colonel and Lily found new quarters at 2400 Sixteenth Street in Washington, D.C. It was here that they first met an eight-year-old girl that would be, for the childless couple, a precious gift. Rose Page, the daughter of a neighbor in the building, was a mischievous, pretty girl who soon had the the solemn Marshall wrapped around her little finger. But it was not to be a one-way relationship, for he demanded high standards of behavior. When one day she greeted him with the well-worn gossip that "a voluptuous Cuban woman" staying in their building was General MacArthur's "sweetheart" (which later proved to be true, except that she was not Cuban but Eurasian), Marshall angrily scolded her.

When a surprised and hurt Rose began to cry, the colonel softened his tone and explained the damage that unconfirmed rumors can cause. Apparently the outburst caused no great harm, for Marshall was to become Rose's godfather, and she would remain close to him for the rest of his life. To him she would always be the daughter that he and Lily could not have. In many ways these were idyllic years for Marshall. He had a happy home life, with Lily by his side after years of long separations, and continued work at the right hand of the army chief of staff, a man whose goals he shared and who treated him as a friend as well.

But in 1924, Pershing, his retirement near and well aware that his protege's advancement required direct command of troops, offered him duty with the Fifteenth Infantry Regiment in Tientsin, China. This was one of the few worthwhile postings in the ever-shrinking U.S. Army, which by now barely numbered 130,000 men.

The end of the 19th century had seen a weak China wracked with internal strife. Outside powers, big and small, hovered waiting to take advantage of the situation. In 1901 China's empress secretly encouraged the Boxer Rebellion, a grass-roots effort to rid the country of the occupying troops controlling parts of China. The Boxers executed hundreds of foreigners indiscriminately, something their home countries could not tolerate. So Germany, France, Japan, England and the United States, among others, sent troops to stop the slaughter. Alarmed, the empress abandoned the Boxers to their fate. Without the support of the central government, and with little more than swords and spears at its disposal, the rebellion collapsed. To assure no repetition, the foreign powers demanded the right to station their troops in compounds that would become known as the Foreign Concessions. Within each concession, the only law was that of the occupying country. The Chinese were not only forced to accept these humiliating terms, but were made to pay for them as well, including that symbol of hated foreign intrusion, the Shanghai park sign reading "NO CHINESE OR DOGS ALLOWED."

Lt. Colonel Marshall's assignment was as second in command of the Fifteenth Regiment. The China posting was viewed as a choice one, especially by army wives. The perks were great, servants were practically free, the treasures of China could be bought for a song and even junior officers could live like kings. However, there was also the filth, poverty and hunger of the people, as well as the instability and danger resulting from the general hatred of foreigners. Or the country's never-ending power struggles—the possibility of being killed was a real one.

In 1924 North China, where Marshall was posted, was controlled by three warlords: Marshal Chang Tso-lin, the ruler of Manchuria; Marshal Wu Pei-fu; and General Feng Yu-tsiang, who not only held the balance of power, but in an ingratiating gesture to the foreigners, became a Christian. Feng wanted to increase the goodwill of the foreigners by mass-producing converts, so he baptized his uncomprehending troops with a fire hose. The rest of the country was in similar clutches, with Chiang Kai-shek's ruling Kuomintang (Nationalist) party trying hard to hold on to its power bases in southern China. The central government was powerless, so anarchy reigned everywhere.

No sooner had Marshall arrived than he was put to the test. Feng, in one of his frequent turnabouts, had abandoned his ally of the moment, freshly defeated Marshal Wu. Wu's troops were fleeing Chang's now-victorious soldiers. Not unreasonably, Wu's men attempted to find refuge—and possibly booty—in Tientsin, something the Concession troops, American and others, could not countenance. Tientsin was, after Shanghai, the second most important commercial center in China. Located some 130 miles from Peking (Beijing), it sat astride a vital railway.

To turn away Wu's men, who grossly outnumbered his meager forces, Marshall had to resort to guile and bluff. He deployed his regiment to guard the railway stock and to deflect the armed mob of soldiers from the city. To the latter end, he stationed well-stocked kitchens at the main entry roads and by dint of persuasion and threats, convinced the armed, leaderless rabble to eat and move on.

In one form or another, this scenario would be repeated often during the next few years until an invading Japan assumed control of the country. But even while the Japanese occupied China, the Chinese would continue to fight each other until 1949. Only then would the mainland be unified under Mao Zedong, the leader of the Communist forces.

Marshall recognized part of the problem in a letter to Pershing: "How the Powers should deal with China is a question almost impossible to answer. There has been so much wrongdoing on both sides . . . there is so much of bitter hatred in the hearts of these people and so much important business interests involved, that a normal solution can never be found."

The irony was that over 20 years later Marshall would return to undertake the very task he now deemed futile—the outcome again sadly proving his earlier observations.

In spite of everything, Marshall's three years in China were happy ones for him and Lily. He learned Chinese and made every effort to absorb the culture and understand the country. He was proud of his activities with his soldiers and the fact that through his efforts in creating recreational facilities for the troops, the Fifteenth Regiment relinquished its long-held distinction as the unit with the highest incidence of venereal disease in the U.S. Army. Using Mongolian ponies, he also organized a mounted infantry unit, which was in good humor referred to as the "Foot Hussars," and did a good deal of riding himself—something he would continue for the rest of his life.

In late 1926 Major Joseph Stilwell was assigned a batallion commander to the Fifteenth Regiment. As General "Vinegar Joe," he would be Chiang Kai-shek's mentor and nemesis in World War II. He and Marshall became good friends, though it seemed an odd pairing. Marshall was clean, precise, careful and ramrod straight; Stilwell was rumpled, profane and slouching. They did shared several traits, though. Both men were perfectionists in their work, flexible in their thinking and pragmatic in their goals. So the two could get along, and they did.

In the summer of 1927, Marshall was posted to the Army War College in Washington, D.C., as an instructor. The China tour over, Marshall and Lily bid the Orient goodbye and returned to the States. But in Washington disaster struck. Lily became ill and was hospitalized. On the morning of September 15, she was told she could go home the following day. When the doctor left she began a letter to her mother, but after a few lines the pen slipped from her fingers. She had suffered a fatal heart attack.

While delivering a lecture at the War College, Marshall was summoned to the phone by a guard who remained with him during the call. "He spoke for a moment, then put his head on his arms on the desk in deep grief. I asked him if I could do anything for him," the guard remembers, and he replied, "No, Mr. Throckmorton. I just had word my wife, who was to join me here today, has just died."

Lily Coles Marshall, the flirt of Lexington, and the love of George Marshall's life, was gone. For Marshall, the homebody who doted on his semi-invalid wife as though her physical limitations were never a burden, acceptance did not come easily. When his sister rallied to his side, he took her help numbly. Even after she removed his many pictures of Lily, leaving only two, he still wandered forlorn around the house, as if looking for his partner. The shock was not over quickly and indeed seemed severe. Marshall's heartbeat became erratic, he lost weight rapidly and for a while he sank into deep depression.

Realizing his pain and his need, his friends and the army offered help. Henry Stimson, the newly appointed governor-general of the Philippines, asked Marshall to join him there as his military aide. Chief of Staff General Summerall offered him three choices: Stay at the War College; go as chief of staff to an army corps (the army's largest formation, composed of several divisions); or go to Fort Benning, Georgia, as assistant commandant of the Infantry School.

Marshall decided on Fort Benning, arriving in October. There he was head of the Academic Department and in a position to implement many of the ideas and objectives that he and Pershing had talked of. These included the ability to simplify, respond and adapt to circumstance; to be flexible; issue commands that are clear and concise, for the battlefield is no place to have to decipher an elaborate message; understand your terrain and the temper of your men; lead by example, not rank; be willing to delegate and then trust those to whom you have given authority. Throughout his life these objectives would remain of primary importance—as would his concepts of honor, duty and country.

It was not simply ideology and philosophy that Marshall would impart. He would drill into his students the lessons taught by the Great War—all the while remind them that the next conflict was not likely to be a repetition of static trench warfare. As he saw it, the next war would be one in which the swiftest weapon, the airplane, would be used first. Then other weapons, the slower ones, would come to support and consolidate the field advantages air power had created. He would teach his students that no branch of the army could function well alone, that it was the successful interaction of all branches that brings victory.

For years lessons at Fort Benning had been taught using exercise books with specific, correct answers given at the back of the texts. Not only that, even enemy responses were a given, as though battles were set-pieces. Marshall did away with the practice. "Expect the unexpected," his dictum went, "and in so doing, be prepared to react *when* it happens, not later, for by then circumstances might have changed once more."

As head of the Academic Department, he was ruthless with his faculty. Those that did not come up to par were quickly weeded out. The result was that in his five years at the Infantry School, he would turn out as fine a crop of officers as Major John F. Morrison had in his days at Fort Leavenworth. And just as graduates of that great teacher proudly wore the label of "Morrison Men," his faculty and pupils were known as "Marshall Men." Their names are a fair roster of the cream of army leadership in World War II; Omar Bradley, later Chairman of the Joint Chiefs; Mark Clark, who conquered Italy and who later became defeated Austria's Allied High Commissioner; George Patton, the driver of tank armies and hero of the Battle of the Bulge; Joseph Stilwell, who kept Chiang

Kai-shek fighting the Japanese instead of his fellow Chinese; Joseph Collins, who as chief of staff would later have General MacArthur serve under him; Maxwell Taylor, another further army chief of staff; Walter Bedell Smith, Bull, Cook . . . the roll call goes on and on.

It was at Fort Benning that Marshall began his fabled "black book." In it were the names of officers who impressed him. Years later, when asked if he also kept one for the incompetents, his answer was brisk as always: "There wouldn't be room."

In 1928 Marshall's mother died. Within the year, Lily's mother died too. One by one the links with the past and with Lily were broken. To forget, he worked hard, tried to be social, took up gardening and pestered the officers at the post with his entertainments. These ranged from the Benning Fox Hunt, which he founded, to setting up treasure hunts that included adults as well as children. Legend has it that he had been seen on horseback in a Japanese kimono, wearing a Filipino hat and carrying a bird cage—all the booty of a successful treasure hunt.

And then he received a fateful invitation to dinner in nearby Columbus, Georgia. When Marshall arrived, only his civilian hosts, Mr. and Mrs. Tom Hudson, were there. The other expected guests were an old college friend of Mrs. Hudson's and her daughter, neither of whom Marshall knew. The friend had been widowed some months earlier when her lawyer-husband had been murdered in Baltimore by a dissatisfied client. Katherine Tupper Brown arrived with teenaged Molly, her daughter, in tow. With some light banter, Marshall and Mrs. Brown began to get acquainted. She was impressed with this man who had a "way of looking right straight through you." After dinner Molly left with a friend, and later in the evening Marshall offered to take Mrs. Brown back to the home of the friends with whom she was staying.

After about an hour in the car, Mrs. Brown remarked that he must not know his way around Columbus very well, for it hadn't taken her nearly as long to get to the Hudsons'. To that, Marshall replied that if he hadn't known Columbus well, he couldn't possibly have avoided her street for so long. Smitten, he called the next day and invited her to a reception at Fort Benning. He sent his car to pick her up, but at the reception did not introduce Katherine to anybody. When she asked why, he explained he wanted her all to himself. Flattered and pleased, she was obviously happy with his attentions.

It is often said that a person's second mate is a replica of the first. In this case the opposite was true. Whereas Lily was a southern belle, Katherine Brown, a southerner herself, hailing from Kentucky, was anything but. The daughter of a prominent "hell, fire and damnation" Baptist preacher, she shocked her family when, after graduating from Rollins College, she left for England and became an actress. One night, exhausted, she collapsed onstage. She fled back to the States and was packed off to the Adirondack Mountains, where clean air and rest would work wonders. Clifton Brown, an old friend, courted her there and asked to marry her. She accepted and settled into being the wife of a successful lawyer. They lived comfortably in Baltimore and produced three children. Life seemed easy and predictable until, in the hallway to his office, Brown was shot and killed by a client enraged over his bill. Molly, the oldest child, was most affected, so Mrs. Brown took her for a long tour. It was at the end of that journey that she had arrived in Columbus.

From the moment Katherine left Georgia, Marshall peppered her with letters. He invited her to return to Columbus. At the end of this next visit, it was plain to both that this was no mere friendship. Katherine, though, wondered how her sons would take to Marshall. By now, Molly was already fond of him.

The solution was to invite him to spend the summer with them at their house on Fire Island. Clifton, 15, was not concerned, but Allen, 12, was against the invitation. "I don't know about that, we are happy enough as we are," he told his mother. The next day he had a change of heart, writing to Marshall, "I hope you will come to Fire Island. Don't be nervous, it is OK with me." He signed off with, "A friend in need is a friend indeed. Allen Brown."

Things must have gone well, for Marshall stayed for five happy weeks. The couple decided a quiet October wedding would befit their status as widow and widower. Pershing was to be Marshall's best man, and only family and a few close friends were to be invited. On October 15, 1930, large crowds, who had gotten wind that General Pershing would be there, packed the Emmanuel Episcopal Church. In truth, neither groom—nor bride—was wholly displeased.

With a warm, loving wife by Marshall's side, the big house at Fort Benning could now feel like the home that he had longed for. Katherine plunged into this new world with gusto. They would remain at Fort Benning for two more years. Then in June 1932, Lt. Colonel Marshall was transferred to a line command again. This time he would head a battalion of the Eighth Infantry at Fort Screven, Georgia, some 18 miles from Savannah.

On his arrival Marshall was greeted with a slovenly post and surly men. It was not without reason this base was called the rear end of the army. In spite of these circumstances, he was delighted with his assignment and proceeded to remedy the faults he saw. He laid out vegetable gardens and ordered the erection of hog pens and chicken coops in order to supplement the rations of the garrison. Meanwhile he had the mess officer increase the lunch portions and directed that married enlisted men be allowed to buy that meal for their families at cost. To ensure the quality of army chow, he and Mrs. Marshall often made a point of sharing meals with the soldiers.

While army bases suffered from ever-tightening budgets, most of the nation was even worse off. It was reeling from the worsening impact of the national economic catastrophe known as the Great Depression. Unemployment and despair dominated much of America as factories shut their gates and farm foreclosures drove more people into the cities—only to be added to the lists of the jobless. Under these conditions Presidents Herbert Hoover and, later, Franklin Roosevelt, viewed the army more as a national police force to handle potential insurrection than as a deterrent to external aggression.

In the early 1930s a desperate Roosevelt initiated the CCC, the Civilian Conservation Corps, as a measure to get unemployed youths off the streets and working on public projects. The corps was to plant trees, build firebreaks, clear national parks, beaches and battlefields, build cofferdams and fish ponds, and learn soil conservation techniques. Chief of Staff General MacArthur suggested the army train them. After some hesitation Roosevelt agreed. By getting the army involved, MacArthur prevented several thousand officers from being furloughed.

George Marshall trained units of the Civilian Conservation Corps with great skill in the 1930s (George C. Marshall Research Library)

At Fort Screven, Lt. Colonel Marshall was originally assigned 500 CCC workers. Most were skinny city boys with sallow complexions and bad teeth, the result of too little food and too much living in slum shadows. Their furtive eyes and defiant attitudes were not enough to hide the ignorance and fear lurking behind them. Marshall's first task was to build the boys up, both physically and emotionally. He fed them well, saw that their rashes and bad teeth were taken care of and gave the illiterate lessons in reading and writing. The 500 CCC workers soon swelled to 4,500, spread over 17 camps in South Carolina and Georgia.

In May 1933 Marshall was notified that he was to have his long-yearned-for eagle. He would again be a full colonel, his last wartime rank. In June he assumed command of the entire Eighth Infantry Regiment. His new headquarters were at Fort Moultrie, South Carolina, in the middle of Charleston Harbor.

Katherine had not yet fully unpacked when Marshall was abruptly transferred to Chicago as senior instructor in a disintegrating Illinois National Guard. The order came directly from MacArthur, whose normal tour as chief of staff had been extended by the president for one year, partly because of the good job the army was doing with the CCC. Marshall appealed to MacArthur, but the chief of staff was adamant, calling him the best qualified colonel in the army for the task.

An unhappy Marshall arrived in Chicago. He hated city living and the Illinois National Guard Division was in sorry shape. His first step was to set an example. He would not allow any slack in the performance of duties. But as his officers soon discovered, he would accept new and different ideas with enthusiasm as long as he felt they benefited the army. In 1936, at the end of three years, he left, satisfied that his purpose had been accomplished.

His new posting on the West Coast would bring a promotion; of that he was sure. But his pleasure was mixed with apprehension. He was now 55 years old. Because of the army policy of retirement at age 64, this left barely nine years for any further advancement. This meant that if he was to reach his long-cherished goal of becoming army chief of staff, he had to be nominated before 1940. In October of 1936, Mrs. Marshall, returning from a trip to Canada, walked in while the phone was ringing. An officer asked her for "General Marshall." Another hurdle in Marshall's career had been cleared.

As a new brigadier general, he was given command of the Fifth Brigade of the Third Division in far-off Vancouver Barracks in Washington State, close to Portland, Oregon. Only one thing marred Marshall's happiness. While still on the family's cross-country trip on their way to the post, the old irregular heartbeat that had bothered while at the War College flared up again. At first he did not think much of it, but once in Vancouver Barracks he was forced to take it seriously. After tests at the base, he was sent to a hospital in San Francisco. There, in December 1936, a diseased thyroid gland was removed. The operation was successful; the heart irregularity stopped, and he regained much-needed weight. Delayed gossip eventually carried news of his illness all the way to Washington, D.C. Concerned, for he already had Marshall in mind for a higher post, General Malin Craig, the new army chief of staff, wired him: "HOW IS YOUR CONDITION. ARE YOU FIT?" By now, Marshall could reply with full confidence, "IN SPLENDID CONDITION. NEVER FELT BETTER."

Again healthy, Marshall could now devote his energies to one of the projects that intrigued him most. Along with his brigade and its "air force" of four obsolete Curtiss biplanes, Marshall had also inherited 33 CCC camps. There he again saw first-hand the two most demoralizing issues facing the CCC train-ees: illiteracy and bleak futures. On his own, he devoted special attention to getting the boys schooling and jobs.

On June 20, 1937, the outside world knocked gently on the doors of isolationist America and of General Marshall. Three exhausted Soviet fliers, having just completed the first nonstop transpolar flight from Moscow to the United States, suddenly landed at Vancouver Barracks airfield. It was not much past 8 A.M. that Sunday—and Marshall had not been expecting com-pany. Quickly, he made arrangements for the men to bathe, rest and eat at his house. He then contacted the wire services, the Russian embassy and the local dignitaries. Soon banquets, a parade and all the other ceremonial paraphernalia were in place. That same morning he called on Portland merchants across the river to get the disheveled and rumpled pilots civilian clothes. By afternoon the men were fitted and present-able. Again, he demonstrated his own advice: to be ready for the unexpected.

While the fliers' visit was peaceful and friendly, the rest of the world was not in quite the same mood. Germany under Chancellor Adolf Hitler was rapidly rearming and establishing what was already being called the Third Reich. In Italy, dicta-tor Benito Mussolini at last had his trains running on time. Spain was torn by a brutal civil war, with Russia and Germany using Spanish soil and blood to test new weapons. Stalin had just purged his army of tens of thousands of its officers in the name of Communist purity; at the same time his factories secretly worked with Hitler's generals in developing better and more lethal tanks. Japan, after swallowing Korea and Man-churia, kept gobbling up huge chunks of China while the Chinese warlords continued to kill each other.

The French, secure in the assumption that they had the best army in the world, smugly prepared themselves to fight the Great War over again. To ensure their success, they built the Maginot Line along their eastern border, which faced Ger-many. It was a steel plate and reinforced-concrete version of the Great Wall of China. Like that ancient border guard, it consisted of a series of fortifications capable of withstanding the heaviest of bombardments. Also like the Great Wall, it would soon prove nearly useless in keeping out the invader. Britain simply *knew* that as long as no one successfully challenged her mastery of the seas, no ill deed could befall her empire. America went Britain one better. With a huge ocean on each side, a good navy and weak neighbors above and below, what had she to fear?

A few Americans thought otherwise. Unfortunately, almost to a man, they were nearly all soldiers. Each time they raised the issue of preparedness, their words fell on deaf ears. For the army's chiefs of staff, from Pershing to MacArthur to Craig, the result of their appeals and warnings had been the same. The country did not want to hear them. But the world was changing, and like it or not, America was going to have to change too.

In July 1938, after two years in Vancouver, Marshall was summoned to Washington, D.C., by the chief of staff to head the War Plans Division of the General Staff. He was not pleased about the assignment, although he had been told it would lead to his becoming the deputy chief of staff, which happened in October 1938. Marshall had his eye on the chief of staff slot, and knew full well that the way there was not through the deputy's door. He also knew that the last opportunity he had to get the chief of staff post was as the immediate successor to General Malin Craig. Otherwise he would be too old to complete his four-year term before the mandatory retirement age of 64. Little did Marshall know that once made chief of staff, he would in fact serve over six years, longer than anyone else. However, that still lay in the future. What Marshall also did not know was that there were powerful people in the capital who already had their eye on him, and were in fact considering him for chief of staff.

Pershing, as always, was on Marshall's side. But there also were others, including the one who would count most: President Roosevelt. The president was aware of Marshall's existence and capabilities. However, the chief of staff post has great political significance; it is not purely a military assignment. Even though in theory it should be, of necessity it also must reflect the army's thinking, and in turn the government's policy. And few men are, or have been, as aware of that as Roosevelt.

Roosevelt was also sensitive to the fact that, as time passed, the world situation was becoming not only more perilous, but also increasingly ominous for democracy. The few nations that were thriving were all under totalitarian regimes. Their leaders, against great odds, had brought prosperity to their peoples—and were clearly committed to military conquests. The democracies, on the other hand, were having a difficult time economically and were plagued with substantial internal political unrest or opposition.

The president's choice for chief of staff was ostensibly among 33 generals. In reality it boiled down to five, Marshall among them. In November 1938, with the European and Far Eastern situation worsening steadily, Roosevelt summoned his army chiefs to the White House. He proposed the manufacture of 10,000 airplanes and in the process the creation of thousands of jobs. His goal, of course, was to sell most of these planes to the Allies—which would not improve the army at all. This left the chiefs, who had been pleading for a balanced force that could be quickly mobilized, aghast. Even General "Hap" Arnold who headed the Army Air Corps was stupefied. When finished, the president asked each for their comments. To Marshall's surprise, most bit their tongues and agreed with Roosevelt. When he came to the deputy chief of staff, Marshall responded, "Mr. President, I am sorry, but I don't agree with that at all." Stung, Roosevelt terminated the meeting.

Marshall later recounted that as the generals were leaving, "They all bade me good-bye and said that my tour in Washington was over." The event was reminiscent of Marshall's forthright initial encounter with General Pershing in the First World War, which witnesses had also deemed disastrous to Marshall's career.

But Marshall's tour in Washington was not over. A few months later, in April 1939, Marshall was summoned to the White House. After some pleasantries and a brief discussion of events, Roosevelt came to the point. He had made up his mind. He told Marshall that he was his choice for army chief of staff. To that, Marshall responded that he wanted to be able to always speak his mind, and it would not always be palatable. "Is that all right?" "Yes," the president replied. The soldier insisted, "You said yes, pleasantly, but it may be unpleasant." With a smile Roosevelt acknowledged it. Then, with the words,

"I feel deeply honored, sir, and I will give you the best I have," the newly nominated chief of staff departed.

Still, it was not until September 1, 1939 that Marshall was sworn in. While that date would always mark for him the attainment of his professional goal, the rest of the world would remember it for a wholly different reason.

September 1, 1939 was the day that Hitler had chosen to unleash the full fury of his Stuka dive-bombers and his rumbling Panzer tanks into a hapless Poland. World War II had begun.

5

PRELUDE TO PEARL HARBOR—AN AMERICAN DISASTER

The attack on Poland introduced the world to a brand new word, one that was to strike fear and desolation into the hearts of millions, soldiers and civilians alike: *blitzkrieg*, literally, "lightning war" in German. A whole new concept of warfare was born. Speed and firepower were its hallmarks.

The basic premise is simple. Use the airplane, here the Stuka precision dive-bomber, to attack and destroy communication and supply centers. At the same time send speeding armored columns of tanks, the dreaded German Panzers, to penetrate deep into enemy territory, bypassing any static fortifications the opponent presents. Have the Panzers followed by motorized infantry and artillery. These engage the enemy's front-line troops, while the Panzers, their initial task completed, wheel and attack from the rear. Meanwhile, have heavy bombers dump their loads on civilian population centers as well as on strategic targets such as military headquarters, munitions dumps and other installations.

The intended effect of the blitzkrieg is to crush the enemy's forces decisively before they have a chance to rally fully. The goal is to create such immediate and total confusion that the enemy's national will to fight is quickly broken. However, in order to accomplish this effect, staggering levels of organization, discipline, production and ingenuity must first be achieved. Supply columns bringing fuel, food, ammunition, maintenance parts and personnel must keep up with the advancing forces. The supply formations in turn need to be supported by rear-echelon dumps and warehouses. Even earlier, the planes and tanks must be designed and built, the cannons and rifles cast and bored, the uniforms for the troops sewn, the boots and helmets cobbled and stamped. Men must be recruited housed, fed and turned into soldiers. In addition, the nation must be rallied to support the effort. Ahead of it all, an organization must be set up to plan for the efficient utilization of the resources mustered. And that organization must also, before the plan is put into action, study and evaluate the unforeseen alternatives that battlefield conditions will inevitably present to alter the chosen plan of action.

If the Allies were to prevail against the Germans, they too would have to organize similarly in order to master this new type of warfare. These were tasks that Marshall, as the new chief of staff of a nation heading for conflict, would have to accomplish. And he would be starting with nearly no resources to speak of—the clock of impending war ticking impatiently all the while. One advantage was that the president recognized the coming menace, although his view of how to handle it did not coincide with Marshall's. Disadvantages included a Congress reluctant to face the possibility of war and its expense, and a public whose mood was isolationist. Then there was an empty purse, thanks to the Depression, and an army top-heavy with thinking and procedures it should have discarded over a generation before.

In the beginning, the new chief of staff's relationship with the president was not auspicious. The president was fond of calling those about him by their first name. When he tried "George" on Marshall, the general's stony face revealed his displeasure, and Roosevelt got the message. More importantly, while Marshall thought of military need, Roosevelt thought of political viability. Marshall vigorously pursued with Congress and the White House the speedy enlargement of the army, something he saw as vital to the national security. But Roosevelt repeatedly pulled him short, aware of the forthcoming elections and that the country's mood was firmly against military growth. To Marshall, this was playing politics with the future of a threatened America. Later he would come to admire Roosevelt, but in 1939 and early 1940 he saw only a man compromising his beliefs for the sake of political expediency.

Marshall's improved opinion of Roosevelt probably dates from a mid-1940 meeting with the president. With Secretary of the Treasury Henry Morgenthau, one of Roosevelt's trusted advisers, Marshall went to ask for $675 million to expand the army from 172,000 to half a million men. Morgenthau made the actual request. Roosevelt listened to him and, with a wave of his hand, dismissed them both.

"Mr. President," Morgenthau begged, "will you hear General Marshall?"

"I know exactly what he is to say. There is no need for me to hear him at all," was the president's flippant reply. Repressing his fury, Marshall asked quietly, "May I have three minutes?" Surprised by Marshall's controlled vehemence, he agreed. "Of course," then added, "General Marshall." In a lucid presentation Marshall described the military situation in Europe and Asia. He mapped out the dire results for the United States if its presently pathetic army were to face the foes that Britain and France were fighting. Did the president not understand that his political expediency would not sway the enemy from making its move when it found it convenient? That only American preparedness could forestall such a move?

"If you don't do something, and do it right away, I don't know what is going to happen to this country," Marshall concluded. "Thank you, General. And thank you, Henry," was the cold reply. But as they reached the door, he added, "Oh, General, come back and see me tomorrow. And bring me a list in detail of your requirements."

It was none too soon, for a few days later General Heinz Guderian's Panzers pierced through the weaker Belgian fortifications into France. Disdainfully, the German armed forces, known as the Wehrmacht (literally, "defense force"), bypassed the mighty Maginot Line, the cornerstone of the French Army's defenses. Nearly unhampered, the apparently invincible Panzers rolled on to the shores of the English Channel. Then came Dunkirk, and the forced evacuation from battered France of what was left of the British Expeditionary Force as well as some French units, a total of 340,000 men. With the British and French defeat at Dunkirk, Hitler thought Winston Churchill, the British Prime Minister, would sue for peace. This would leave Hitler free for his pet project, Operation Barbarossa, the invasion of Russia. But Churchill did not comply: the French might be vanquished, but the British would fight on.

America applauded the courage of the British and wished them well. Roosevelt was willing to sell arms and supplies to the Allies, but he could only do so under the "cash and carry" conditions Congress had imposed when it passed the Neutrality Act. The trouble was that after 50 nearly obsolete destroyers had been shipped to Britain much of the materiel the Allies wanted and needed had yet to be manufactured. All the U.S. Army had in its warehouses was World War I stock. Britain was not in a position to be picky. So it bought the lot.

But the British, having discovered both the effectiveness and limits of airpower, were most interested in modern aircraft—the very 10,000 airplanes that Roosevelt had asked for earlier, in 1938—and that had seemed such a preposterous proposal to Marshall at the time. The Battle of Britain was raging across English skies, so their need was urgent. With amazing speed, new American factories were opened, and soon warplanes were pouring out—nearly all being shipped to Europe, and a very few going to strengthen Marshall's Army Air Force.

Congress had at last seen the merit of Marshall's continued fight for an enlarged military force. In fact, it approved an even larger appropriation than the army in its current condition could possibly spend. So Marshall's efforts to restructure the army's ossified bureaucracy were redoubled, for he saw that only with a new internal structure could his goals be achieved.

When an all but exhausted Britain declared it had no more gold, Roosevelt and Congress on March 11, 1941 passed the Lend-Lease Act. Under it the Allies were given an open credit line, so their needs could be met—and American factories kept humming. But while weapons went to Europe in quantity, the U.S. Army continued to get only a trickle. To correct this, still more new factories and shipyards were opened, so both demands could be satisfied.

Two forces made selling arms to the Allies acceptable—despite the official status of the United States as a neutral country. The first was that the sympathies of the nation were by and large with the Allies. The second was that for a country still in the throes of the Depression, armament orders meant work, work meant pay, pay meant money to spend—and money to pay others for their work in keeping the plane and tank workers working—the very cycle needed to revitalize the still-lagging economy. So it was British gold and French treasure that towed America back to prosperity. And it was American weapons and supplies, bought with that gold and treasure, that kept the ideals and freedoms of democracy alive in a ravaged Europe. Then, just as America's industrial might reached production levels at which it could begin to deliver to the U.S. Army the supplies Marshall saw as vital, a new player came to the table and Europe's need for armaments suddenly skyrocketed.

In June 1941, Hitler suddenly launched Operation Barbarossa, the invasion of Russia, taking Stalin by surprise. Since the British had not yielded, the two-front war that Hitler's generals feared most had come to pass. Early on, it looked as though the blitzkrieg's effect on the Soviet Union would be a repeat of that in Poland and France. The bulk of the Soviet air force, the world's largest, was caught on the ground and destroyed. The Panzers' advance was at first slowed only by their need to refuel and to replace worn-out tank treads. Hitler's optimism was so great he did not even think of winter uniforms for his troops. He was *that* sure Moscow would be his before the snows came. Russian losses in men and materiel were staggering; entire Soviet armies either surrendered or were annihilated. Grudgingly, Stalin called on America for help. Swallowing its distaste for communism, America agreed to rearm Russia—and extended it Lend-Lease aid as well—while still refusing to get further involved. And once again, with the Russians now coming first in terms of priorities, the needs of Marshall and the U.S. Army had to take a back seat.

Another enemy now loomed: Japan. It would, in fact, unlike the European aggressors, touch American interests directly. In Asia, the United States did not have the luxury of other countries fighting a stong military power while it equipped itself for war. An armed-to-the-teeth Japan was the unwitting legacy of Commodore Matthew C. Perry's black ships. When enterprising Perry in 1853 entered what is now Tokyo Bay to ask for humane treatment for shipwrecked sailors, a coaling station for American vessels and an opportunity to trade with Imperial Japan, he could hardly have envisioned the results his journey would bring to either country less than 90 years later.

For centuries the Japanese had remained a closed society, isolated by choice from the rest of the world. Japan was ruled by a warrior class led by a shogun in Tokyo. The emperor in Kyoto held little more than ceremonial power. When Perry arrived with his side-wheeler warships spewing black clouds of smoke, the peasantry was convinced the "foreign devils" had harnessed volcanoes. Perry was not welcome, but his ships had guns. The Japanese, having nothing to counter them, bowed to the inevitable and concluded a treaty with the United States that yielded to the demands Perry had made. But the lesson was clear. Japan must become strong in the same way its unwelcome visitors were strong: with steamships and factories—and cannons and rifles.

So in a remarkably short time, about 30 years, the samurai warriors gave up their topknots and kimonos and clogs for visored caps, belted uniforms and boots with puttees. Industry was established and Japan prospered. However, while the old agrarian Japan had been self-sufficient, the new industrialized Japan was not. Raw materials had to be obtained elsewhere, and to pay for them Japanese products now needed to find external markets. So, like another island nation—Great Britain—Japan embarked on the path of survival by conquest.

By late 1941 Britain was on its knees, France was divided and Germany had turned on its Soviet partner. Japan saw its opportunity. It had been warily watching the military buildup of America, and it resented the country's anti-Japanese legislation and moves to cut off sales of oil to Japan. It saw the reinforcement of the Pacific Fleet and its concentration at Pearl Harbor as a direct threat to Japanese security, not as the warning Roosevelt intended. The resulting fear and anger drove Japan inexorably to war with the United States.

Marshall was aware of the situation. However, as a soldier he recognized it was troops in the field, not paper armies—which at this point was about all he had—that win battles.

Misjudging the Japanese, Roosevelt and Secretary of State Cordell Hull assumed Japan was going to break off diplomatic relations. Marshall and Chief of Naval Operations Admiral Harold Stark were not so sure. Since July 1941, five months earlier, they had put Panama and the Pacific bases on alert for possible Japanese military action, since, thanks to a new cryptographic, or code-breaking, machine, America had been for some time intercepting Tokyo's diplomatic cable traffic and knew war might be imminent.

In Hawaii, Lieutenant General Walter C. Short, the army commander, had already taken, and reported having done so, all the measures he believed necessary in light of the warnings he had received. Because of the large Japanese population in Hawaii, Short considered sabotage to be the greatest threat. So he parked his planes tail-to-nose and wing-to-fuselage, making the guarded area as compact as possible. Ammunition was double-locked in its dumps, and road patrols were intensified.

A naval or aerial attack on Pearl Harbor was the last thing on General Short's mind. Indeed, because such a scenario seemed so remote, the single radar installation on the island was operated only three hours a day. The general's naval counterpart, Admiral Husband E. Kimmel, shared Short's opinion. Navy planes patrolled the skies every day, for it was assumed the only way to attack Pearl was by ship, submarine or ship-launched aircraft. As for Marshall, he considered the Philippines the obvious target for a full-blown Japanese attack. These mind-sets may explain the mystery about the unpreparedness for the attack.

Then on November 27 came further instructions from Washington:

> Negotiations with Japan appear to be terminated for all practical purposes . . . Japanese future action unpredictable but hostile action possible any moment. If hostilities cannot be avoided, the U.S. desires that Japan commit the first overt act . . . Prior to hostile Japanese action you are directed to take such reconnaissance action and other measures you deem necessary but these measures should be carried out so as not, repeat not, to alarm civil population or disclose intent.

These instructions held two phrases that later many would use against the president and Marshall. The first is *the U.S. desires that Japan commit the first overt act.* When Roosevelt insisted on this unfortunate directive, what he had in mind was avoiding the possibility of isolationists pointing a finger and accusing his administration of starting a war in order to help the British—a fear they had been voicing all along.

The second phrase is the order, *"these measures should be carried out so as not, repeat not, to alarm civil population or disclose intent."*

Of course, what Washington hoped by this last phrase was to not give provocation. It did not want Japanese nationals in Hawaii to inform their home country of reconnaissance and other measures. Such action might be interpreted as an aggressive move by the United States. Ambiguity of purpose clouded the message's objective and confused its recipients.

Unbelievably, Short and Kimmel took no further action, not even requesting clarification. For Sunday, December 7, they had planned an early morning golf game, and their arrangement remained unchanged. But the chain of blunders did not end in Hawaii, but continued in Washington.

For reasons unknown, Chief of Staff Marshall and Chief of Naval Operations Stark had allowed themselves to think that Pearl was on a full war footing. Incredibly, even with radio, telephone and courier communications, no one in Washington was aware that neither Short nor Kimmel—each responding to a different command—had in fact taken the ordered precautions. On Sunday, December 7, 1941, that error resulted in disaster.

Of course, to Marshall the Philippines seemed the prime target for any Japanese attack. American bombers based there could wreak havoc with convoys heading for Indonesia, Malaya or Indochina. Even if Japan was to conquer these lands, it would help the Japanese little, since shipping to or from these areas could be easily intercepted. It was this logical reasoning that blinded Marshall and America. That the Japanese could, in a single blow, seek to destroy the entire Pacific Fleet was apparently beyond conception.

On December 3, code breakers revealed that Japan had ordered many of its diplomats in Europe and Asia to destroy their encrypting machines and papers. This information was passed on to Hawaii. In San Francisco, the Japanese consul managed to set fire to his house while burning his papers. The local Fire Department put the fire out.

On December 5, the aircraft carrier *Lexington* sailed out of Pearl Harbor, heading for Midway with a load of planes for the base there. With its departure all three of the Pacific Fleet's aircraft carriers were now out of Hawaii.

The Japanese First Air Fleet, led by Vice Admiral Chuichi Nagumo aboard his flagship, the carrier *Akasi,* was now fully assembled and steaming to its fateful Pearl Harbor destination. It was a formidable force. The main striking element was a group of six aircraft carriers with 360 torpedo planes, dive-bombers and Zero fighters. They were backed by three battle-ships, two heavy cruisers and three submarines. Accompanying them was a swarm of escort craft and six oilers, so the fleet could refuel at sea—a novel concept at the time. So far the force remained undetected; their composition, location and destination were known only to the Japanese navy.

On Sunday, December 7, 1941, Washington woke up to a cold windy day. There was little question now that war was imminent. Marshall ordered that a message to that effect be sent to all Pacific posts and Panama.

Coordinating his efforts with the navy, he contacted Admiral Stark. Stark offered to send the warning through naval channels, but Marshall said no, the army could handle it. By now it was 11:50 A.M. Washington time—6:50 A.M. in Honolulu—launch time for the Japanese fleet's planes, which were one hour's journey from their target. The message, in Marshall's tough-to-read handwriting, was given to Colonel French of the signal corps. French was successful in getting the cables to Panama and the Philippines out around noon, but Hawaii could not be raised because of atmospheric conditions. Colonel French, ignorant of the navy's offer, opted to transmit the coded message via Western Union instead; its San Francisco transmitter was much more powerful than the army's and could overcome the static—itself an eloquent comment on the nation's view of the army's importance at the time.

The cable arrived in Honolulu at 7:33 A.M. local time. It was sent to General Short via a motorcycle messenger. His name was Tadao Fuchikimi. His journey proved how effective the antisabotage measures were, for being Japanese and thus suspect, he was held up a number of times by army patrols before he could deliver the coded cable.

But Hawaii was not dependent on Washington cables only. The operators of its single radar unit got ready to shut down at 7:00 A.M., as instructed, when they suddenly saw a big array of blips on their screen. They counted no less than 50 planes at the outer limit of their radar's range, just over 130 miles. The signalmen relayed the data to the duty officer at the army air force base. Thinking this was the expected flight of B-17's coming from the mainland, he thanked them and hung up.

The navy, too, received its own private warning—even earlier. At 6:20 A.M. the ancient destroyer *Ward* was entering Pearl Harbor when the supply ship *Antares* reported seeing an unidentified submarine "having depth control trouble" at the harbor's entrance. Verifying the submarine was not an American one, *Ward* opened fire at point-blank range and sunk it. The incident was reported to Admiral Kimmel. Suspecting this to be another unidentified sighting by a nervous crew, Kimmel decided to investigate first and act later. As he hung up the phone he didn't know that his golf date would be canceled anyway.

Within minutes Washington would hear a message, one for which it was hardly prepared: "AIR RAID, PEARL HARBOR. THIS IS NO DRILL."

A somber and anguished Marshall waited to hear from the Philippines. He knew full well, that if they too were under attack, he had no help to send.

6

WORLD WAR II—ARCHITECT OF VICTORY

For most Americans, World War II did not begin in earnest until the early morning of December 7, 1941, Honolulu time.

At 7:55 A.M., with wholly unanticipated precision, bombs and new Japanese-designed shallow-water torpedoes began to rain on the 86 navy vessels anchored in "Battleship Row" and the rest of Pearl Harbor. At the same time the tightly parked planes of the Army Air Force assigned to protect them were strafed and bombed by the carrier-borne attackers. Within two hours the Pacific Fleet was decimated: 18 major ships were sunk or badly damaged, among them seven battleships. One hundred eighty-eight planes were destroyed and 2,330 Americans killed. The three aircraft carriers of the fleet, being at sea at the time, were spared—something that would prove greatly significant soon after. The only other major U.S. vessel absent was the cruiser *Indianapolis.* Four years later she would carry the atomic bomb to the tiny island of Tinian, only to be sunk shortly after by a torpedo fired by a Japanese Pearl Harbor attack veteran.

Like it or not, America was now officially at war. And Marshall, like the German High Command, would be faced with that terrifying military specter: a two-front war.

Some Americans, however, had already been fighting for over two years. An undeclared war had in fact already been under way for some months in the Atlantic. Since early 1941 Americans had been fighting against the European Axis powers, as a Roosevelt memo of June 13, 1940 openly stated:

... The United States active in the war with naval and air forces only. Plane production is progressing to its maximum. America is providing part of the Allied pilots ... American shipping is transporting supplies to the Allies. U.S. Navy is providing most of the forces for the Atlantic blockade.

Marshall, as army chief of staff, was naturally fully aware of these actions—which did not mean that he approved of them. His main concern was the preparedness of American forces, and to the extent that Britain was buying time for the United States, he approved of the aid. But that aid was keeping the American army from becoming battle-ready. Were the Nazis to defeat Britain—a likely scenario at the time—the U.S. Army's mouse would not be ready to face the Wehrmacht's cat.

But Roosevelt, like President Woodrow Wilson before him, was adamant. And as in 1917, U.S. vessels, presumably neutral and as such not permitted to transport war materiel, were in fact carrying supplies and armaments to the Allies. To legally do so under international law would require the United States to declare war on the Axis. Roosevelt, recognizing that as unacceptable to the American public, stopped just short of such a move. However, in November 1940, after his reelection, he felt secure enough to proclaim, "The United States must be the great arsenal of democracy. . . . The Nazis must be defeated . . . It was a matter of most vital concern that European and Asian warmakers should not gain control of the oceans which lead to this hemisphere." These words were heard across the nation a year before Pearl Harbor. To many, they were unwelcome.

What further angered the isolationists, people who felt that the country should stay out of European conflicts, was the loud and obvious sigh of relief with which London greeted the news of the attack on Pearl Harbor. Quite understandably, the American disaster was viewed as a godsend in tottering Britain. At last America could openly come to her aid with *all* her power. And when the sigh was echoed at the White House, Roosevelt became doubly suspect. After all, his imprudent comments at a meeting with Marshall, Stark and his War Cabinet on November 26, 1941 were known to his political enemies: ". . . the Japanese are notorious for making an attack without warning. The question is how should we manuever them into the position of firing the first shot without allowing too much danger to ourselves."

To the isolationists, Pearl Harbor was exactly what Roosevelt had long been working for—an excuse to enter the fray on Britain's side and to go to war with Japan. For the latter idea there was a tenuous connection to fact. Twenty-eight years earlier, in 1913 when he was assistant secretary of the navy, Roosevelt had espoused the concept of a preemptive war against the Japanese, a position he abandoned a few years later. Still, some operated under the mistaken belief that the president, with Machiavellian cunning, had engineered the attack on Pearl to accomplish this. In addition, to a proud America, the thought that ineptitude, ignorance and just plain wishful thinking at all levels played the major role in the disaster was patently unacceptable. So the conspiracy myth was born. While aimed at Roosevelt, it would tar Marshall too and haunt him for years to come.

Monday December 8, 1941, was a strange day in America. Wild rumors were rampant. Mexican-based Japanese bombers had supposedly been sighted over Los Angeles and San Diego. San Francisco reported a carrier force off its shores, and people rioted. Submarine sightings were so numerous that to account for a fraction of them all the navies of the world would have had to be concentrated off California's coast. Just to keep America on its toes, the Japanese did in fact sink a few vessels close to the coastline. A particularly enterprising submarine of theirs lobbed a few shells onto an oil refinery near Los Angeles, causing little damage but great panic. With a few air squadrons and some old coastal artillery, there was little Marshall could do.

In the meantime, events unfolded at dizzying speed. On that Monday, Congress declared war on Japan—but not on Germany or the other Axis powers. Four days after Pearl Harbor, Germany, continuing its nearly unblemished record of diplomatic blunders, declared war on the United States. This move resulted in putting a quickly unified America firmly on the side of the Allies and spared Roosevelt much grief and effort.

By now German-led forces controlled nearly all of continental Europe; the exceptions were the neutral countries, Spain, Switzerland, Sweden and Portugal. Turkey leaned toward the

Axis, but still held out. In Asia, China remained an ineffectual giant, and the Japanese continued their victory parade across Asia.

Marshall's prime thought remained the fate of the logical Japanese target, MacArthur's forces in the Philippines. His worst fears were realized a few hours after the Pearl Harbor attack. The B-17 bombers he had so strongly believed would deter attack had in fact been destroyed while on the ground because of lack of coordination at MacArthur's headquarters. Next Marshall was informed that, as he had anticipated in the exercises conducted with Major General Hunter Liggett in 1916, a strong Japanese force had landed at Lingayen Gulf on Luzon Island and was closing in on the capital, Manila. As his earlier script had predicted, that force could not be stopped with the meager resources that the United States could muster. With his air cover gone, MacArthur's odds, shaky at best, plummeted. To save Manila, he declared it an open city—meaning it would not be defended—and at the end of December 1941, the Japanese marched in and took control.

In Washington, Marshall summoned one of his new generals, Dwight David Eisenhower. Eisenhower had served for three years as MacArthur's chief of staff, so his knowledge of the Philippine situation was vast. Within an hour of his arrival he was briefed by Marshall on the results of the attack. Marshall then abruptly asked Eisenhower, "What should be our general line of action?" Nonplussed, Eisenhower asked for a few hours. "All right," Marshall responded, and dismissed him. What Eisenhower did not know was that Marshall had already reached his own conclusions, and that the query was more a test than a request for advice. When Eisenhower returned, he laid out the circumstances unemotionally: Without transports for troops and supplies, and warships to protect them, any effort to reinforce the beleaguered MacArthur in time was doomed to fail. Marshall concurred: "I agree with you. Do your best to save them."

Then Marshall turned to other pressing matters. He attempted to persuade the Soviets to allow U.S. planes to use Vladivostok as a base in order to bomb Tokyo. Stalin, who had signed a neutrality pact with Japan, flatly refused. Already battered by the Germans on the west, he was not willing to risk Japanese retaliation against his Asian borders.

Still, Marshall would not abandon MacArthur. He attempted to secure shipping by offering huge amounts of cash to skippers willing to risk the Japanese armadas. He even shipped anti-aircraft shells by submarine. But the result would be as anticipated: too little and too late. For all practical purposes, MacArthur was on his own. From the island of Corregidor, his last bastion, MacArthur radioed he was prepared to defend it to the last man. Marshall ordered him to escape to Australia instead, so as to fight another day. A reluctant MacArthur left aboard a torpedo boat, but not before he grandly proclaimed "I shall return," a promise he would keep.

Everywhere it seemed the Japanese were victorious. Part of their success was that as fellow Asians they were in many places hailed as liberators from the white overlords. Thailand openly joined their Greater East Asia Co-Prosperity Sphere. In Malaya and Burma, Indian units went over to the Japanese side. In other places where their arms were challenged, superior military skill and veteran troops made them prevail more often than not.

Once in Australia, MacArthur was named Supreme Commander of All Allied Forces in the Southwest Pacific. This impressive title belied the fact that there were fewer than 32,000 troops in his command, most of them rear-echelon personnel. His air force consisted of about 100 planes, many of them obsolete. Before MacArthur's arrival, most of what would have been his navy had been sunk in the battle of the Java Sea. He thus had the least enviable assignment at the time. The U.S. Navy shied away from his theater; the U.S. Army was barely able to help. Australia and New Zealand's own troops were away, fighting in North Africa, and the Kuomintang (Nationalist) Chinese divisions facing Japanese formations in nearby Burma were of generally poor quality. Consequently MacArthur did not have much to work with, or neighbors to count on. Marshall, however, supported him as much as he could, for he was fully aware that abandonment of these forces would guarantee Japanese control of the South and western Pacific. Like the European theater, this one needed support, too.

Nevertheless, the grand strategy decided on by Roosevelt and British Prime Minister Winston Churchill at the Arcadia Conference in December 1941 remained unchanged: Europe and the Atlantic would have to be won first, then the Pacific. Even with all of America's advantages—resources of man-power, productivity and relative safety from direct enemy attack—Marshall felt the country simply could not cope with a two-front, all-out war. MacArthur would have to make do with what he had.

Marshall was determined in his efforts to increase U.S. production and to turn a civilian industry into the armory of the Allies. He badgered industrialists, cajoled unions and by his directness persuaded a still-reluctant Congress to fund his and Roosevelt's goal—the creation of a strong army. But that would take time. So even though troops in the Pacific would sustain additional casualties and deaths while await-ing reinforcements and supplies, the conduct of the war in its larger scope demanded that Marshall's attention be turned away from the Pacific and focused on the Atlantic and Europe instead.

The Allied strategy indicated that this was the best course to take, but for most Americans the real enemy was Japan. Again, there was not much that Marshall could do until America built enough shipping and the navy regained its strength. After that, the army would in fact be sending about as many men to the Pacific as it sent to Europe, but the bulk of supplies would still be heading across the Atlantic. It would only be after Operation Overlord, the invasion of France June 1944—still years away—that the Pacific front would become a priority.

Meanwhile the German advance on the Soviets had stalled at Stalingrad, and as with Napoleon, the terrible Russian winter began to take its toll on the invaders and their equip-ment.

As Marshall had predicted, the only way out for the Soviets was to draw the Panzers deeper and deeper into Russia; to fight and retreat, leaving nothing but scorched earth to the Ger-mans, and thus stretching the Wehrmacht supply lines to the breaking point. The Soviets were helped by Hitler's miscalcu-lations, which apparently had not taken into account the vastness of Russia, nor its harsh winters and immense popu-lation. Instead of quickly reaching for Moscow, the emotional, political, industrial and communications heart of the nation, the Fuhrer insisted on scattering his forces on other targets.

The Russians, by now included in the Lend-Lease aid, were being resupplied with American materiel and foodstuffs. Unlike the British, though, their attitude was, "We are dying for you, so you owe us all the things we need." Their attitude would get even worse when Germany declared war on the United States.

The German declaration of war only deepened Marshall's dilemma. He knew that Roosevelt and the public would be impatient and clamor to show the Germans and Japanese the might of America. The trouble was that at this stage there was not much military might in America except in Hollywood films and in what was left of the fleet. There was little satisfaction Marshall might get from having "told them so." Instead, he knew the steps he must take before America could deliver a telling blow to either enemy: he had to build up its long-neglected strength.

In the meantime, he approved a daring, if token, raid. Midway was still held by U.S. forces, and three carriers in the Pacific remained intact. On April 18, 1942, led by Colonel James Doolittle, 16 army B-25 bombers took off from the decks of the *Hornet,* 650 miles from Japan, to drop their loads on Tokyo in a gesture of defiance. Since the planes lacked the range to return to their carrier, their crews were instructed to fly on to China, where they would be rescued by Kuomintang forces. The actual damage they caused was minimal, but the psychological shock to the Japanese was great. For the first time in centuries the emperor was menaced, something that they could not countenance.

Keenly aware that Japan as an island nation must maintain control of the sea-lanes if it was to profit from its conquests, Japan's combined fleet proposed to engage what was left of the U.S. Pacific Fleet in a single battle, destroy it and then offer peace terms. American-held Midway Island was the obvious target.

However, through *Magic* code-breakers, America learned of the plan before it was put into action. That knowledge and Japanese overconfidence would bring on June 3–6, 1942 a wholly unexpected and decisive victory to America, one that radically changed the balance of power in the Pacific.

But Midway was to be the only bright spot for Marshall in this period. His main concern was to be left alone by Roosevelt and Churchill so he could create the fighting force that could deliver the decisive blow he envisioned. Churchill, coming from a small nation that depended on its overseas empire for supplies and markets, wanted to fight a war of attrition on several fronts. That this also would allow Britain to maintain control of its empire was a fact that did not escape Marshall. As an inducement to Roosevelt, Churchill dangled the prospect of many victories soon rather than a big one later, something he knew would keep the public happy. Roosevelt was inclined to listen. It was Marshall's job to counterbalance Churchill's eloquent entreaties.

America, however, was not Britain. Even if unprepared, it still was a self-sufficient nation with plentiful resources and a huge population. It had the ability to muster a mighty army and with it, to deliver a single fatal blow. The plan Marshall proposed and Churchill opposed was simple, but its execution was not: Build a great army, ship it to England, have it invade France and destroy the Wehrmacht. That done, transport the now veteran troops to the Pacific and attack the Japanese islands in force. But the first half of this plan, conceived in 1941, would not come to pass until 1944, much of that delay caused by Churchill's fragmented approach. To fill the needs of this force, Marshall had to recruit, train, equip and transport several million men. He had to organize the industrial establishment to support them. Not only did this army's manpower grow to be overwhelming, it was equipped with the latest and best weapons—a superabundance of materiel that dazzled its allies, disheartened its enemies and spared the lives of many G.I.'s.

Marshall did not want to deploy military resources in a piecemeal fashion—precisely what Churchill was urging Roosevelt to do. Marshall had to constantly fight both leaders, whose focus, understandably enough, was first on political, not military, objectives. In that effort he would have an unexpected ally. His name was Field Marshall Sir John Dill, formerly chief of the Imperial General Staff, now serving as chief British liaison officer in Washington. From their first meeting late in 1941, the two men hit it off and became good friends. They had a clear understanding of each other's problems, thought alike, and had come to trust one another. When Dill brought a British issue to Marshall, he knew that he would get a fair hearing and a straight answer—and, if Marshall agreed, his strong support.

Neither forgot that one served Britain and the other the United States—yet both realized that their countries shared a common objective—to win the war—and that was the goal they unstintingly worked for.

Roosevelt liked to play his cards close to the vest, so frequently his messages to and from Churchill regarding military matters were not made available to the army, leaving Marshall in the dark. Churchill, on the other hand, kept his troops well informed—which of course included Dill. It was often through Dill, receiving his reports from London and sharing them with Marshall, that Marshall kept abreast of Roosevelt's plans.

It was this kind of political, devious behavior by Roosevelt that gave Marshall much of his clout with Congress. After many hearings, Congress realized that the general would speak the truth however unpalatable, and that he would not yield to popular pressures for the sake of expediency. It also found that he would arrive exceedingly well briefed on any matter about which he would speak. When that was not the case, Marshall would bluntly say so, and offer to return when he felt better equipped. Most important, he was truly nonpartisan, a vital point with a Congress dominated by Republicans but with a Democrat in the White House. Neither the executive or legislative branch had much trust or love for the other. When asked about his political coloration, Marshall would respond, "My father was a Democrat, my mother a Republican, and I am an Episcopalian," for he had a deeply held belief that soldiers should stay out of politics.

Like the officers of most countries, his outlook was essentially conservative. And like many of them, he refused even to vote, lest that be assumed an indication of partisanship. With a man like this, a Republican Congress could vote even for things Roosevelt wanted—without appearing to bow to the White House. "Congress always respected him and would give him things they would give no one else," remarked House Speaker Sam Rayburn after the war's conclusion. And like Congress, the public came to trust Marshall. Clearly he was a man without political ambition or a desire for self-aggrandizement, a man whose whole effort was devoted to one purpose: the security of America.

No other figure in the country commanded as much respect and trust. In 1944 *Time* magazine honored him as the "Man of the Year," an accolade it would repeat in 1948. In an editorial, *Life* magazine proclaimed, "the folks have confidence in this general because he never forgets the folks." Roosevelt's White House secretary wrote, "Wherever this man goes, he inspires reverence, may God spare him." These were fair reflections of America's feelings about him. To the British military and to Churchill—who were initially unimpressed by the modest American general—would come the realization that here was a man with a strong conscience, yet one whose rectitude did not stem from self-righteousness or ignorance. Churchill, who had no love for generals, came to view Marshall as a statesman and to respect him as such, calling him "the Organizer of Victory." At home, when, for the next two trying years the news from the front would more often be bad than good, Marshall was the one symbol around whom Americans of every political persuasion could freely rally.

With Pearl Harbor painfully fresh on his mind and with America now at war, Marshall felt it imperative that the army be restructured. There was a need for vigorous combat commanders, men willing to assume the initiative and not waste time covering their rears. Mercilessly he retired officers whom he did not feel would be effective and replaced them, often with younger men. Many of the displaced colonels and generals felt betrayed and lost. But there was a war to be won, and the deadwood had to be removed before the task could proceed in earnest. His "little black book," where for years he had been jotting down the names of officers of promise, became an object both of fear and hope to the officer corps.

Some of the new men would be as old as he or even older. Some would be ones he personally disliked and found difficult. But nearly all would vindicate his military judgment in the days to come. While the British promoted and demoted their generals with sometimes dizzying speed, few of the American commanders Marshall chose proved disappointing.

At the Arcadia Conference in early 1942, Roosevelt decided Marshall's cross-channel strategy was best. Surprisingly, Churchill agreed. But the British also wanted General Erwin Rommel's Afrika Corps dealt with. No sooner had the conference's strategy been agreed upon than the British renewed their push for their Mediterranean strategy, describing it as a blow to the "soft underbelly" of the Axis. The plan was to land in North Africa and then attack weak Italy instead of fortified France. A dubious Marshall ordered Eisenhower to lead the American forces in the invasion of North Africa and in the long trek that would have them crossing the Mediterranean and working their way up the Italian boot. However, the "soft underbelly" turned out to be exceedingly well protected. It was many months before Allied armies could exert pressure on the German homeland from that theater. And it would be in Italy, not far from one of the bloodiest and most contested battlefields of the war, that Marshall would encounter personal tragedy.

Both of Marshall's stepsons had enlisted in the army. Aware of Marshall's attitude toward nepotism, they kept their relation to him secret. After graduating from Officer's Training School, Second Lieutenant Allen Tupper Brown was posted to the First Armored Division as a tank commander and shipped first to North Africa and then to Italy. He survived the bloodbaths at Monte Cassino and Anzio, but on his way to Rome, on May 29, 1944, a sniper ended his young life with a single shot.

His mother, as all mothers in such circumstances, was devastated. Marshall, who while Allen was in the army had steadfastly refused to lift a finger to improve his lot, for a brief moment turned into just another grieving father and husband before returning to his role as a stern soldier.

As the war progressed and Britain's strength was sapped by war losses, it became more and more obvious that Operation Overlord, the planned invasion of Europe, was to be an American show backed by its Western allies. As such, it became a given that its commander would be an American. The obvious choice was the army's chief of staff, for not only was he the best known and most tried, but the project had from its inception been his brainchild.

While the Allies had all along assumed the forthcoming Allied Supreme Commander would be Marshall, an assumption shared by the general himself, U.S. public opinion became polarized on learning of this possibility. Some felt he would perform the task brilliantly and that the command would ensure his rightful place in the history books. They recognized that field duty had always been Marshall's first choice, so they saw it as the only fitting reward for this warrior. Others viewed the command as a demotion, and waxed indignant. Their sentiment was shared by many who felt that with Marshall in

Europe the high command would suffer at the moment when its steadiest hand was vital. Besides, there was the Pacific War yet to be won, and Marshall would be needed there too.

Roosevelt as usual waffled on the subject—after all, it was his decision and a difficult one. If Marshall had asked for the post, no doubt it would have been his, but the general's pride and modesty prevented that. When Roosevelt finally asked him pointblank, Marshall replied that he was a soldier, and would serve at whatever post he was assigned. It was a noble answer, for it was no secret that he would have loved to follow in the footsteps of his mentor and friend, General Pershing. The president finally chose Eisenhower, whom Marshall had recommended. Roosevelt softened the blow by telling him, "I could not rest easy with you out of Washington," a sentiment most of the country shared. Marshall's disappointment was huge, but with iron will and granite self-control, he said nothing; and went to work making Eisenhower's new task as easy as possible.

Again, as in World War I days, it was the excellence of Marshall's work in central planning that had once more kept him from a field command. Should something go amiss and the mighty army he had forged founder, then his hand would have been absent from the tiller. This neither America nor the president could allow to happen.

On D Day, June 6, 1944, the mighty armada Marshall had so hard worked for, one greater than any the world has seen, set sail from Britain. Its destination: the beaches of Normandy, in northern France. Aboard were the first of 39 combat divisions, half of them American, the rest British, Canadian, French and Polish. Aloft was a fleet of over 2,000 transport planes and gliders carrying airborne troops. Softening up the German defenses, 2,200 bombers dropped their loads on enemy positions, and the naval guns of the warships escorting the invasion force began firing. As the Allied infantry landed and overran the fiercely defended beaches of the French shore, the death knell of Hitler's Third Reich began to toll. But that bell would toll somberly for quite a while. Nearly a full year would pass before Hitler died and an exhausted Germany finally surrendered.

For Marshall, though, it would be time of great vindication. (Later in the year, in December 1944, he would be appointed

The initial U.S. assault on Omaha Beach in Normandy, France. Without Marshall's brilliant planning, D-Day might very well have failed (Library of Congress)

General of the Army, with five stars.) The generals he had chosen to lead, from Dwight D. Eisenhower to Omar Bradley to George S. Patton, all performed brilliantly. Yet the German resistance was so determined that it would take until August 1944 to finally break out of France. In December 1944, the Allies were momentarily stopped in the Ardennes in Belgium and Luxembourg in what would be called the Battle of the Bulge. The last German offensive on the western front, it cost U.S. troops heavy casualties. Finally on March 7, 1945, Allied forces crossed the Rhine and entered German soil at Remagen.

Then, on April 12 1945, Franklin Delano Roosevelt died, plunging the nation into mourning. For Marshall it was a great loss. The two men, who at the beginning had been wary of each other, had over time built a strong relationship based on mutual respect, if not friendship. Hearty Roosevelt and taciturn Marshall had been the two pillars around which America had rallied to fight this war, and now one of them was gone. Roosevelt would miss the final victory, the victory for which he had done so much and that now loomed near. Eleanor

Roosevelt, in a moving tribute to Marshall and her husband's collaboration, asked the general to take care of the funeral arrangements. A feisty former haberdasher from Missouri became president. In time Harry S. Truman would rise to a measure of greatness, but for the moment he was the uninformed, ill-prepared ex–vice president of the United States, now thrust into a wholly unexpected role.

Meantime, the Russian onslaught advanced mercilessly. It pushed the Wehrmacht out of Russia, Poland, Romania, Yugoslavia, Hungary and Czechoslovakia. Soviet troops banged on the gates of Vienna and entered the city—the first sons of the steppes to do so since the time of Attila the Hun. But their march did not stop there. Like a giant thresher, they mowed down German resistance in a line stretching from the Baltic to the Alps. But the Wehrmacht stubbornly fought on.

In Berlin and in Hitler's headquarters at Wolf's Lair, coups were attempted by German officers who saw the only prospect for their nation's survival in the elimination of the Fuhrer and on a negotiated peace. Their efforts met only with failure and savage reprisals.

With the Allies closing in on all sides, the end finally came in Berlin on April 30, 1945. Hitler put a bullet through his brain. His body, together with Eva Braun's—his mistress of years and wife of merely hours, who had also committed suicide—were incinerated by SS guards. Two days later, Berlin fell to the Russians. On May 7, 1945, Germany surrendered. World War II in Europe was over.

All eyes then turned eastward, toward Japan. Two strategies, each endorsed by a different service, were activated. The navy's plan attacked via the Central Pacific, while Marshall chose the southern route. Both proved quite effective, but at great cost. Like the German soldier, the Japanese soldier was highly disciplined. But in addition he had a code foreign to the West: death was better than capture and dishonor.

Recognizing this fanatic tenacity, Roosevelt had extracted a promise from Stalin at the Yalta Conference in February 1945. Within three months of the defeat of the Nazis, Russia was to declare war on Japan and attack Manchuria. This was a vast and rich region of Japanese-held China that provided much materiel for war and whose possession had always been a Russian objective. With Stalin's promise, Roosevelt hoped to minimize the inevitable American losses that would result from the invasion of the Japanese home islands, to date the only apparent way to finish the war.

By May 1945, Japanese power had waned. Still, the Americans were hoping to find a way to end the war.

Ostensibly, there was only one. The atom bomb.

7

THE ATOMIC BOMB AND THE
SOVIET MENACE

The European conflict over, Marshall could now concentrate on the Pacific theater. When viewed from a strictly military basis, the war there had recently been going well. Step by step, island by island, the noose around Japan had grown tighter, choking all but that country's fighting spirit. For America, though, the price of its victories was becoming too high. The Japanese, in their determination to die rather than surrender, were inflicting extremely heavy casualties.

A grave concern was the thought that if this unbending resistance was so stubborn at the outposts of the empire, it would be even stronger when the Allies reached Japan's home islands. If the fierceness of fighting increased, the number of American lives lost would increase in proportion. On paper the United States had about 6 million troops to be deployed. Opposing them were some 5.5 million Japanese soldiers. While many of the latter were rear-echelon troops, their ability to carry on prolonged guerrilla warfare was not in question. In fact the Imperial Inner Council foresaw a 20-year war of attrition in which their forces never surrendered, and at the end of which the exhausted invaders cut their losses and left Japan.

In Washington three proposals had been advanced to conclude the war with Japan, one from each of the services.

The navy wanted to establish a blockade and thus starve Japan into submission. Since the island needed imports—both of foodstuffs and materiel—the concept seemed to make sense. However, it did not take into account the character and determination of the Japanese people. These had already been demonstrated by small units and even individual soldiers who months after their positions had been overrun, still continued to fight, often living on berries, roots and little else.

The Army Air Corps felt that saturation bombing would conclude the war in short order. Its commander, General Henry (Hap) Arnold, wanted enough aircraft in fields close enough to the enemy homeland to be able to obliterate the defenseless cities, since for all practical purposes, Japanese airpower had ceased to exist. What this plan neglected to take into account was that in Europe the approach had repeatedly failed in spite of thousand-bomber armadas pounding German cities day and night. Hamburg, Dresden and Berlin, nearly pulverized, held on. And prior to that, from Guernica to Helsinki to London, the bombed cities' will to go on did not waver. In fact, if anything, this will to continue fighting seemed to be strengthened by the bombings.

The army saw invasion as the only workable approach. Given the nature of the Japanese, it would by far be the costliest and most arduous road, but as Marshall learned long ago, only infantry, by taking physical possession of the enemy's strongholds, can in the end clinch victory. Unfortunately, this scenario carried a horrendous price tag: an estimated half to one million American casualties as well as the unspoken specter of a war that might last for years to come.

But another way, a new way, now appeared not only viable, but desirable: the atomic bomb. It would obliterate tens of thousands of lives and everything else in its path in one single stroke. That is, if it really worked as expected.

The whole atomic issue had its beginnings in 1938, when two scientists in Nazi Germany announced that barium was one of the products of their bombarding uranium with neutrons. While earlier experiments, notably those of Italian physicist Enrico Fermi, had also split the uranium atom, the process had never yielded more than a little energy. What Otto Hahn and Friedrich Strassmann had done was to demonstrate an approach whereby the energy released was great enough that a chain reaction could be started and maintained. It was this self-sustaining event that made the harnessing of nuclear energy—and an atomic bomb—a distinct possibility.

This information was relayed to Niels Bohr, a Danish physicist who was preparing to leave for Washington, D.C., to attend a conference on theoretical physics. There he joined Fermi, who for five years had been looking for just such a breakthrough and who had earlier migrated to the United States. They both immediately recognized the terrifying military potential of such a development in the hands of a man like Hitler. For months they unsuccessfully tried to convey their concern to the U.S. government through normal channels. Finally, Bohr and Fermi wrote a letter to President Roosevelt, enlisting the help of Albert Einstein, over whose signature it was posted. To emphasize its importance, they arranged not only to have it hand-delivered on October 11, 1939, but to have it actually read aloud to him as well:

> . . . it may become possible to set up a nuclear chain reaction . . . by which vast amounts of power . . . could be generated. . . . This new phenomenon . . . could lead to the construction of . . . extremely powerful bombs of a new type. . . . A single bomb of this type . . . might well destroy an entire port together with some of the surrounding territory. . . .

On hearing the missive's contents, the president called his military advisor, General Edwin "Pa" Watson, handed him the notes and said, "This requires action."

But it would not be until February 1940, four months later, that with a check of $6,000, the U.S. government committed any resources to atomic research. And ironically enough, it would be on December 6, 1941, the day before Pearl Harbor, that the S-1 Committee of the Office of Scientific Research and Development was formed under Dr. Vannevar Bush, the president's scientific advisor. Its four other members were vice president Henry Wallace, Secretary of War Henry L. Stimson, Dr. James B. Conant, president of Harvard University, and General Marshall. The committee's purpose was to study the viability of building a nuclear bomb. It would take nearly four years, 2 billion dollars and the work of nearly 100,000 for the army, which was entrusted with the task, to confirm that it was possible and then to accomplish it. General Marshall put the builder of the Pentagon, General Leslie Groves—a man with a can-do reputation—in charge and gave him nearly dictatorial powers. Although it may not have been the aim of some of the civilian scientists involved, the clear purpose of the program was to produce the most awesome weapon mankind had ever known, and to do so before the Germans could.

The French and British had their own atomic programs under way—and, of course, so did the Germans. The isolated Japanese, while advancing more slowly, were nevertheless making strides in that direction. And the Russians, even though without as yet a substantive program of their own, were kept well informed by their spies of the other nations' nuclear efforts—particularly the newly combined Anglo-American one known as the Manhattan Project. Foremost among Stalin's informants was Klaus Fuchs, a German-born British subject secretly acting as liaison with London. Fuchs would faithfully continue at his double task, working for both the British and the Russians, until well after both atomic bombs had been dropped.

Thus, by 1945, the possibility of a nuclear weapon, while unknown to the masses, was recognized by the scientific and military leadership of all warring parties. What no one would know until the actual explosion was the extent of its immediate destructive power, or its long-term consequences. Japanese scientists had concluded that no country could possibly have a bomb ready in time to affect the outcome of the war. Japan's leaders would therefore be caught unawares and would seem incapable of understanding the devastation unleashed on Hiroshima. Whatever chance they might have had to stop the dropping of the second bomb would disappear with their shocked inability to react quickly enough to the first one.

Decisions about the use of the bomb had already been made. In what was called the Hyde Park Agreement of September 1944, Roosevelt and Churchill concurred that the atomic bomb "must after mature consideration be used against the Japanese who should be warned that this bombardment will be repeated until they surrender." While it may seem callous to attack first and warn later, this decision should be viewed in the context of wartime conditions and animosities.

Roosevelt would of course be dead by the time the bomb was ready, and another hand would be in charge of the country—and of the fate of Japan. When Vice President Harry Truman was informed by Mrs. Roosevelt on the afternoon of April 12, 1945 that he was now president of the United States, his knowledge of the Manhattan Project was next to nil. This was not surprising, since Roosevelt had made certain that Truman was kept as far away from the White House as possible, having no love for the "little haberdasher" and former senator from Missouri, a product of the useful but despised Pendergast Democratic machine that ruled politics in that state.

Marshall, however, viewed Truman differently. Two years earlier, when Congress had appointed the Truman Committee to oversee the ballooning army expenditures in order to cut waste and fraud, Marshall had ordered that full cooperation be extended to the Missourian. He found that in fact Truman performed the problem-laden task honestly and with distinction.

For his part the then senator trusted Marshall—so much so, that after Roosevelt's death, Britain's Ambassador in Washington, Lord Halifax, wrote to an anxious Churchill that the new president "venerates General Marshall"—thus reassuring the prime minister that no extreme policy changes need be expected.

But one change was in the offing and it was a big one. Unlike Roosevelt, Truman was an ardent anti-Communist and had little love or trust for the Russians, particularly Stalin. He already had a view of the postwar world, and the Soviet role, as he saw it, loomed much too large for his liking. To do anything about it, though, he needed a trump card, for while the Americans at the end of the European war had raced out to Asia, the Russians had instead consolidated their positions. Truman knew, as did Stalin, that the American public wanted peace, that it was in no mood to reengage in a European war should the Soviets prove intransigent in their demands, or refuse to honor their commitments. This was his frame of mind when he left in July 1945 for the Potsdam Conference, convened essentially to divide the spoils of war.

During the conference, where Truman was meeting with Churchill, Stalin and De Gaulle, he was told via coded telegrams about the successful tests of two nuclear devices. America, and only America, now had atomic capability, and with it the trump card Truman thought he needed to keep the Soviets in line.

The big question now was how to use it. At first it was generally assumed that of course the bomb would be dropped on Japan as Roosevelt and Churchill had agreed at Hyde Park. But then dissenting voices arose, at first timidly, then with greater force. The original purpose had been to keep such a terrible weapon from being used by the Nazis. But with the defeat of Germany, they argued, that goal had been accomplished. Others proposed to share the knowledge with all—the Soviets included, a notion that a horrified Truman rejected outright.

Then there was Japan. Was dropping the A-bomb really necessary to force Japan to surrender? Had not the Japanese already been making peace overtures, asking only that they be allowed to keep their home islands and continue to be governed by their emperor?

It wasn't only pacifists or idealists who asked these questions. The army, the navy and the Army Air Corps, for differing reasons, all opposed the first use of the bomb on an occupied target. However, political considerations, mainly Truman's desire to rein-in Russia, prevailed over the military's judgment.

Admiral William Leahy said that "the bomb would be of no material assistance" because the Japanese were ready to surrender. In his memoirs he amplified this by adding, " . . . by being the first to use it we had adopted the ethical standards common to barbarians in the dark ages." General Eisenhower, at a lunch with Truman and General Omar Bradley on July 20, 1945, expressed his opposition to using the bomb against a Japanese city. General Curtis LeMay, head of Bomber Command, somewhat optimistically predicted that the Japanese would surrender by October—without the use of the bomb.

Marshall did not feel as confident about Japan's willingness to surrender, as he stated at a meeting on May 29 with Assistant Secretary of War John McCloy. The general nevertheless opposed the use, without notice, of an atomic weapon: "Every effort should be made to keep our record of warning clear. . . . We must offset by such warning methods the opprobrium which might follow from an ill-considered employment of such force." Secretary of War Stimson backed his position. However, the suggestion was overruled by the president.

Even earlier, Marshall had asked for a demonstration on a deserted island to which Japanese observers could be brought as a vivid means of showing the might of the bomb. Barring that, he called for bombing an evacuated Japanese naval base or manufacturing center. Both ideas came to naught.

Another thought was to target an empty site in an area within Japanese control and so inform Tokyo, but that too was overruled. One fear was that the Japanese might concentrate American prisoners of war in the area. Another was that the bomber could be shot down and its cargo captured. Still another consideration was the unthinkable scenario in which—with the whole world watching—the bomb might fail to explode. Better not to announce than to give succor to the enemy and be embarrassed.

The most vocal advocates for the bomb's use against a populated target were Truman's new secretary of state, James Byrnes; General Leslie Groves, head of the Manhattan Project; and Grove's top scientific subordinate, J. Robert Oppenheimer, who declared that there was no safe way to demonstrate the bomb's might—other than by destroying a city. By way of consolation, he added that the blast should not produce more than 20,000 casualties.

Perhaps the foundations for the use of the atom bomb lay first with Allied insistence on unconditional surrender, a concept that arguably lengthened the war unnecessarily, and then with basic decisions made by Roosevelt at Yalta, and later on by Truman at Potsdam.

Both the Yalta and Potsdam conferences involved the Russians as the other major players. At Yalta in February 1945, the Allies caved in to Soviet territorial demands in exchange for their promise to enter the war against Japan within three months after the end of the European conflict. Until then, Stalin had carefully avoided any act of aggression against the Japanese, recognizing that any such act would condemn him to a two-front war, the very factor most responsible for the Nazi defeat. He would continue to follow this policy until the Potsdam Conference in mid-July of the same year. By then the United States had nearly exhausted Japan. However, the last thing Stalin wanted was to face victorious American troops on Japanese possessions bordering the Soviet Union. So he aimed to get there first.

It could be argued that with the European war over, with or without American blessing, Stalin was going to wheel about and grab Mongolia and reestablish control of Sakhalin Island. The island, once entirely Russian territory, had been divided between Russia and Japan in 1905. Russia wanted to avenge the humiliating defeats, including this loss, which she suffered during the Russo-Japanese War of 1904–1905. Stalin also felt a weakened Japan would be incapable of holding onto lands bordering on Soviet territory. In short Stalin and Russia could well profit immensely from the postwar situation.

Certainly General Marshall had no illusions regarding Stalin's motives. Yet at the time of Yalta, the containment of Soviet expansionism into Eastern Europe, never mind Japan or China, was not a major issue for most in the United States. And as mentioned before, with the European war over, the mood in America by mid-1945 was to be done with Japan as quickly as possible. The country yearned for a quick return to the more comfortable isolationist position, a thought that disturbed Marshall greatly.

So when it became clear that one, possibly two bombs would be ready by the summer of 1945, the news was viewed as heaven-sent. U.S. troops would not die needlessly; the Russian bear would be tethered by fear of American atomic might; and demobilization would take place as rapidly as troops could physically be brought home. That Mongolia would in any event go to Russia and that Eastern Europe would remain under Stalin's control were not in doubt. By waving the bomb, though, the United States hoped that further Soviet encroachment would be checked without the involvement of American troops. Thus, the successful and peaceful beginning of the Pax Americana was to be assured.

What the United States did not know, however, was that Stalin was fully aware of the progress of the atomic project. Much of the information that would make a Soviet bomb possible within four years had already been transmitted to Moscow—this was true even before Truman informed Stalin and Potsdam that the bomb was now a reality. History will later bear witness that, of the anticipated American goals—independence for Poland and the other Eastern European nations, peace in Greece and China, a neutral Korea—only one, early demobilization, would be achieved within the decade.

Like Roosevelt at Yalta, Truman too had been outfoxed by Joseph Stalin.

In the meantime, Stalin was fully aware that the Japanese were asking him, as their partner in the Russo-Japanese Neutrality Pact, to present the conditions under which they were willing to surrender to the Allies. Were Tokyo to do so, he feared his plans for Far Eastern conquests might be thwarted, so Stalin kept silent. Meanwhile his overloaded troop-trains unceasingly rolled eastward toward prized Mongolia. He did not know that through American cable intercepts, Truman was well aware that Japan's insistence on keeping the emperor was now essentially their sole condition for surrender. For Truman, though, the Japanese were now a secondary concern. What mattered most was thwarting Stalin's goals. And what better way to show the awesome strength of America's hand than by obliterating an entire enemy city and its inhabitants in seconds.

In Germany in mid-1945, the Allies issued the Potsdam Declaration. It devoted but a single paragraph to the question of Japan—basically reiterating that unconditional surrender was the empire's only option.

By broadcast and leaflet, the Potsdam Declaration was made known to Japan. Its emphasis on unconditional surrender had an effect opposite of that intended. It strengthened Japan's will to fight to the bitter end. Even the pacifists found the terms unacceptable. To the Japanese it was unthinkable that the emperor not be recognized. So Tokyo, viewing this as another propaganda barrage, decided to *mokusatsu* the warning. This is a Japanese colloquialism, which translates into "ignore" or "issue no comment"—two very different concepts. Insofar as the president of the United States was concerned, however, the warning had been delivered. And Marshall, good soldier that he was, carried out his orders.

On August 6, 1945, on the tiny island of Tinian in the Mariana Islands, the Enola Gay, a B-29 bomber named after its pilot's mother, was prepared for its 1,400-mile flight to Japan. It was loaded with "Little Boy," an unarmed and partially assembled uranium bomb. The plane flew toward its destination in the early morning light undisturbed. At 8:15 A.M., the first atom bomb was released from the bomb bay of the

A view of the destruction wrought by the atomic bomb in the city of Nagasaki
(George C. Marshall Research Library)

aircraft over the city of Hiroshima. Within moments, close to 100,000 people would perish.

In a burned-out Tokyo, Japanese leaders were at first numbed by the reports of total destruction, and they again failed to respond to the American demand for unconditional surrender. On August 9, three days after the bombing of Hiroshima, a second bomb—the last in the U.S. arsenal—was dropped on the city of Nagasaki with similar results. Finally, on August 14, the Japanese emperor told his shocked and war-weary people that he had agreed to the Allied terms for surrender. World War II, the greatest conflict in the history of the world, was over at last.

8

CHINA'S BITTER RICE

With World War II over, and after 49 years and nine months as a soldier, George C. Marshall longed to settle in a place that he could permanently call home. Like most army officers, his quarters had always been temporary, lasting only as long as a given posting. Dodona Manor in rural Leesburg, Virginia, had for a few years now been his short-term refuge, the place where for a weekend or a few days, he could forget Washington. During the war Mrs. Marshall had the old but graceful Federal-style building redone at great expense—and at the substantial risk of incurring the general's ire when the cost was found out, for he was a parsimonious man. But now at last he could fully savor the advantages her care had lavished upon Dodona Manor. On arriving in November 1945, he was tranquil and appreciative when he and Katherine stood together on the porch looking over their land.

Only a day before he had still been army chief of staff. Then, in a brief and moving ceremony, a grateful Truman and nation accepted his request to be allowed to step down. The president described him as "the greatest military man this country has produced," and with a typical touch of defiant hyperbole added, "or any other country." Telegrams and letters arrived from all over the world echoing those words and paying tribute to the self-effacing man whom Churchill had called "the organizer of victory."

Now Quarters One at Fort Myers in Virginia lay empty and silent. For six years the big brick house had been the Marshall home. Soon it would be redecorated to fit the taste of General Eisenhower, the new army chief of staff, the man Marshall had handpicked as his successor.

On the very day of Marshall's arrival at Dodona Manor, a tired Katherine Marshall headed upstairs for a before-dinner nap. As she walked up the steps, the telephone rang. The general answered it. After a very brief conversation, he hung up. An hour later, refreshed by her nap, she came downstairs. Before she could ask him who the caller was, she heard on the radio that Ambassador Hurley had abruptly resigned and that General Marshall had been appointed by the president as special envoy to China. The announcer added that the general was to leave immediately. Katherine's anger and consternation were plain. The general explained that the call had been from the president. "He asked me if I would go to China for him, and I said yes." And he added, "But I could not bear to tell you before you had had your rest." His words did little to mollify her. She felt betrayed by Truman, for she had understood that with her husband's resignation would come the end of Marshall's public life—a life that had unarguably exacted a toll on the general, even if his habit was not to complain of it.

A month passed before his departure, perhaps the most trying month of his life until then. Congress was holding hearings and an investigation into Pearl Harbor. Marshall suffered the humiliating experience of being questioned about his motives by a Congress and a nation that until a few days earlier, he had served as a soldier so unselfishly and so well. By way of excusing Congress, he would later say, "The investigation was intended to crucify Roosevelt, not to get me."

In the end the investigating committee's six Democrats and four Republicans concluded in their majority report that there was no malevolent plot or obvious dereliction of duty—other than the actions of Admiral Kimmel and General Short in Hawaii. A minority report disagreed. On his last day of testimony, a tired but proud Marshall left the Senate Caucus Room—and the audience, more perceptive than the committee about what the nation owed this man, stood up and applauded him as he exited.

A few days later a C-54 army air force transport left for China with Marshall aboard. A whole new crew surrounded him. Earlier Katherine had offered to go with him, but the general, aware of the turmoil and discomforts of a China on the verge of full-scale civil war, regretfully said no.

Marshall's task was to seek a solution or accommodation whereby the Kuomintang and the Communists could at least agree not to tear China apart. Truman feared that if a full-fledged civil war materialized, the Communists would win—and even worse—the Russians would quickly move in and take over. Those fears drove Truman to send Marshall to China; it was felt he was the only man who could work the miracle. Marshall's only chance of success rested in having the Kuomintang's (Nationalist's) Chiang Kai-shek take the steps needed to better the life of his people—not just of his top party members. Without this, Chiang could not hope to overcome the grass-roots movement the Communists controlled. What Marshall did not as yet know was that his only leverage with Chiang Kai-shek—the threat to cut off his American supplies—could only be used as a bluff, for neither Truman nor James Byrnes, his secretary of state, were willing to take such a step.

The other problem was that while there was no way to force Chiang into line, there was no incentive for the Communists to cooperate either. U.S. aid to them—filtered through the Kuomintang—was little more than a laughable idea to Mao Zedong, the Communist leader. Mao had seen how weapons and money that had been shipped from the United States to Chiang and destined for use in the war against the Japanese had not been used for their intended purpose. But Truman had been deluded by China's supporters in the United States into thinking a coalition possible. They led him to believe two impossible things. One was that the puritanical Communists would be willing to accept political, military and economic control by the corruption-ridden Kuomintang. The second was that Chiang would relinquish any power in order to induce his opponents to do so.

Marshall was thus put in the untenable position of being a mediator and at the same time having to rule on one side's favor—the Kuomintang's—and this before either side presented its case to him personally. To make matters worse, the winner pre-selected by Washington was unwilling to compromise, unable to govern and thoroughly corrupt.

The troubles that Marshall had been dispatched to solve had deep roots. In the 19th century the ruling Manchu emperors had been unsuccessful in controlling the southern provinces of

China—as well as in stopping the encroachment of foreign powers on Chinese territorial integrity. Then came the brief, disastrous Sino-Japanese War of 1894, when a defeated China was forced to recognize the independence of Korea and to cede Formosa (Taiwan) as well as other lands to the victorious Japanese. In addition, a large indemnity had to be paid to Japan as well. A bankrupt empire had to turn to foreign banks that demanded territorial, mining and railway concessions as guarantees for their loans. It was to safeguard these investments that foreign troops were first stationed on Chinese soil. The unsurprising result of this insult to Chinese sovereignty was the 1901 Boxer Rebellion, with the ruling dowager empress joining the rebels in advocating the killing of all foreigners.

Foreign troops put down the uprising—an act that accentuated the xenophobia of the frustrated Chinese. Despite their impotence, the Chinese saw themselves as superior beings and foreigners, whether American, European or Japanese, as godless barbarians. With the consequent exposure of the impotence of the Celestial Empire, the imperial political system itself began to be seen by some Chinese as unacceptable. Whereas the old system involved political intrigue that eventually resulted in simply replacing one ruler with another, the idea of a different China with a wholly new political system began to take hold.

But years would pass before this could happen—and in the meantime, China became more and more fragmented as the power of the central government, now in the hands of a boy-emperor and his regents, precipitously declined. Province after province declared its independence from Machu rule. Not surprisingly, civil war broke out, and Sun Yat-sen, the leader of the main revolutionary group, was elected provisional president of the Republic of China on December 29, 1911.

Decades of strife were to follow, for at its birth the republic had been fatally mortgaged. First, the new republic tolerated only a single political party—Sun Yat-sen's Kuomintang. Then there were the warlords of old with their large standing armies. They tightly controlled their territories and joined whoever offered the highest price for their services—their loyalty in effect shifting in response to market conditions. Marshall would see the disastrous consequences of this kind of government firsthand when he served in China in the 1920s. Also in the 1920s, the Bolsheviks, having gained control of most of Russia from their political enemies, began to view their turbulent next-door neighbor as fertile ground for the exportation of communism and sent their agents to proselatize. A ready audience awaited them, but it had strong ideas of its own, ideas which clearly did not include Russian domination over Chinese affairs, something Truman later failed to understand.

It was clear that in order for the republic to survive, an essential element would be a national army answering solely to the central government. Only then could actual central control be achieved. To that end Sun Yat-sen founded the Whampoa Military Academy—whose first commandant was a fiery young officer named Chiang Kai-shek, fresh from a stay in Russia. Quickly Chiang became one of Sun's most trusted lieutenants. Sun also took in many Communists into the Kuomintang, while being careful not to identify himself with their goals.

At Whampoa, Chiang created the clique that would later help him rule China, a clique that for a time included a substantial number of Communists. On the death of Sun in 1925, Chiang became the head of the Kuomintang army. Not long thereafter he took as his second wife Soong Mei-ling, the United States–educated sister-in-law of Sun Yat-sen. Her charm, intelligence and powerful family connections in China and the United States would prove great assets to Chiang's ambitions. As he increased his control of the Kuomintang, he began to distance himself from the Communists, even though for a while in 1926, Mao Zedong, the Communist leader who some 23 years later would expel Chiang from China, uneasily served as the Kuomintang chief of propaganda. Mao soon saw that the two ideologies were mutually exclusive, an argument reinforced by the fact that Chiang executed any Communists caught threatening his position—a courtesy Mao reciprocated.

During these early years, Mao established his power base with the peasantry, while Chiang depended for his strength on the loyalty of his lieutenants and the troops they commanded. As long as the numerical odds were overwhelmingly in the Kuomintang's favor, clashes between the two generally found Mao the loser.

However, there were now other problems. In 1931, Japan invaded Manchuria and steadily worked its way southward into North China proper. Grumblings but little else followed from the other powers. Since both Chinese factions were embroiled with each other in the south, there was little either could or would do to stop the invaders.

This situation would change in 1934–1935, when Mao, after losing several battles to Chiang, expelled his Soviet advisers and led his defeated troops on the Long March, their trek from Juichin in Kiangsi Province to Yenan in Shensi Province, a 6,000-mile walk to the north. Of the 90,000 or so who started out with him, fewer than 10,000 made it to Yenan. The rest died along the way. Constantly harassed by vastly superior Kuomintang forces, bombed on a nearly daily basis and moving through thinly populated mountainous terrain, Mao's troops took nearly a year to reach Yenan.

Supported by the local population, Mao then waged constant guerrilla warfare against the invading Japanese. When the enemy moved deeper into China, Mao urged Chiang to fight them, going so far as to have him kidnapped in Sian and forced at gunpoint to agree. For the duration of WW II a truce was declared between the Communists and the Kuomintang. But even after his agreement, Chiang would seldom commit his best troops and equipment to fight the Japanese—when he would fight them at all. His concern was always to save his men and materiel for the time when he would face Maoist formations. With the defeat of Japan, Chiang thought his chance had at last come.

At the end of 1945 the Kuomintang, mustering between four and five million men, got ready to use the huge store of armaments the United States had provided. Rich with materiel and commanding a vastly larger army, the generalissimo was convinced he could not lose. After all, the Communists had only about 300,000 soldiers, little artillery, no air force, no navy. Confident of his superiority, Chiang prepared to attack.

By now Washington had at last lost some of its naivete about China, and realized that thanks to corruption, lack of training and poor leadership, the Kuomintang army was in fact a very expensive paper tiger. Chiang had the soldiers and the guns, but his men fought for loot and to avoid the lash. The Communists, or Chicoms, as they were called, on the other hand, fought for an idea. Koumintang troops "liberated" their needs—be they food, shelter or women. Unlike them or the warlord soldiery, Mao insisted that his men pay for whatever they took from the civilian population; so more often than not, the peasants cooperated willingly. For the peasantry, long resigned to looting and rapine—and little interested in ideology—this was enough to win their support.

On his arrival in China in 1945, Marshall's fears were confirmed. Chiang had taken on all the trappings of a despotic ruler. Worse, his troops were unreliable, and the corruption of his officers rampant. Somehow the generalissimo had convinced himself that Marshall was there to aid him, so he placed a new list of demands for materiel. He wanted trucks, tanks, planes, ammunition, fuel, food, uniforms—more and more supplies. With these, he vowed, victory would quickly be his. U.S. Army General Albert C. Wedemayer, who replaced General "Vinegar Joe" Stilwell as Chiang's adviser and commander of U.S. troops in China, confirmed Marshall's judgment of the poisonous political and military conditions the Kuomintang had created.

At first taken aback by Marshall's threat to cut off aid, the generalissimo made a few concessions. This brought Chou En-lai, Mao's second in command, to the conference table. But the distrust each side felt for the other was palpable, the result of too many broken promises and betrayals on both sides. For three months Marshall worked to find a path of understanding and trust. For a while it even looked as though he might succeed. Armed with what looked like an agreement, albeit a tenuous one, he left for Washington in March 1946, to arrange the financing needed to implement it. The two biggest obstacles, the integration ratio of Kuomintang to Communist soldiers in the new national army, and the matter of Manchuria, had apparently been resolved.

In Washington he spent a month in a whirlwind of meetings arranging for credits for China—and, if that were not enough—having to attend further congressional hearings on Pearl Harbor. In China meanwhile, his fragile truce was crumbling. Manchuria, occupied by the Russians since late 1945, was being happily looted by them. Wishing no interference, the Russians refused to allow U.S. Marines or

Kuomintang soldiers to disembark at any of the ports they controlled. When they finally left—taking with them the industrial machinery the Japanese had installed—Mao's troops rushed in to fill the void. So Manchuria, the most heavily developed part of China, was now under Communist control, a clear violation of the Marshall accord. For his part Chiang had not been idle. He had been arresting the Communist members of the truce teams who were to monitor field disputes. In China, things were back to normal.

Expressing a sentiment that in all likelihood Chou En-lai shared, Mme. Chiang wrote Marshall, "I feel that I should tell you frankly that your presence is vital . . . even the short time you have been absent proves what I repeatedly have said to you—that China needs you."

Some weeks later Marshall returned, this time with his wife. By now, positions on both sides had hardened. Communist generals, well supplied with armaments left behind by the Japanese in Manchuria, arrogantly predicted further victories and refused to consider compromise. The Kuomintang armies, for once well led and reasonably disciplined, began their attack on Manchuria. Faced with Chiang's successful offensive, Chou once again accepted the possibility of a compromise, but by then Chiang, feeling what victory was nearly his, was only interested in a military solution. Marshall told him his victories were illusory, for the enemy was simply withdrawing, forcing him to extend his supply lines and thinning his ranks as it lured Kuomintang armies into covering more and more territory.

In May 1946 Eisenhower arrived, ostensibly on a military inspection of U.S. troops in China, but in reality carrying a message from Truman to Marshall. The president, tired of Secretary of State James Byrnes acting as though he owned the White House, offered Marshall the secretaryship. The plan was that as soon as Marshall was ready to return, Byrnes was to become "quite ill" and resign. Marshall accepted the assignment, but felt he first must complete the task at hand.

For the next seven months Marshall continued his efforts to bring about reconciliation to China. Time and time again he cajoled one party to come to the conference table only to find the other no longer interested. The only time anyone was

Marshall poses with Chiang Kai-shek (to Marshall's immediate right), Chou En-lai (to his immediate left) and other dignitaries in China (George C. Marshall Research Library)

willing to negotiate, it seemed, was while their side was losing. As soon as the roles were reversed, the parties changed their positions accordingly. Marshall attempted to build trust with the Communists, only to find they had little faith in U.S. promises. Hampered by Truman's directive that control of China must remain in Chiang's hands, he had little to offer Mao other than personal assurances. Truman, Marshall knew, would not accept other than a secondary role for the Communists. In Washington, meanwhile, Marshall's efforts to force Chiang to compromise were thwarted by a strong "China Lobby" that still believed in the myth of the Kuomintang's virtuous and patriotic resolve. Marshall could see the Communists rapidly gaining, while a grossly overconfident Chiang continued to predict victory in a few short months—provided the Untied States stepped up deliveries—which it obediently did, little realizing that the supplies would shortly be in Communist hands.

Finally, on January 7, 1947, after over a year of incredible frustration, Marshall returned to Washington. He had little more to show for his time in China than an enduring friendship with Mme. Chiang, a friendship Katherine Marshall warmly shared. His efforts to broker an impossible peace accord would not only go unrecognized, but within a few years these efforts would be used to impugn his character and denigrate his achievements.

9

THE MARSHALL PLAN

On January 21, 1947, General George Catlett Marshall was confirmed as secretary of state by the Senate. He was the first career soldier to assume the post. The confirmation process took less than an hour. Queried earlier by the press about his political affiliation, he only admitted to being a soldier and an Episcopalian, his usual response. To further clear the air, the morning of the confirmation he flatly stated to reporters, "I am assuming that the office of Secretary of State is nonpolitical . . . and I am going to govern myself accordingly . . . I cannot be drafted for any political office."

This should have calmed any fears the Republicans might have had that by cooperating with him, they might be grooming a potential Democrat for president. This was no idle speculation. The vice presidency was vacant—the result of Roosevelt's death and Truman's becoming president—and the Constitution designates the secretary of state the successor to the president until new elections are held. Also, for both Republicans and Democrats, the elections of 1948 had to be considered. Obviously Truman was not interested in creating a possible competitor for his party's nomination. Marshall's statements thus reassured the president as well.

For a beleaguered Truman, Marshall's arrival was not a moment too soon. The congressional elections in November 1946 had brought the Democrats a resounding defeat—the loss of 9 Senate seats and 55 House seats was hardly welcome news to Truman. Obviously the nation and the Republicans who now controlled Congress wanted some changes made—quickly. One change they welcomed was the replacement of Secretary James Byrnes with Marshall. Byrnes, a master politician, had nevertheless managed the near-impossible: to be detested by the Republicans and to be rejected by his own president.

With the war over, the mood of the nation was becoming strongly isolationist. The American people wanted to forget the war. They wanted lower taxes and no foreign adventures to support, financially or otherwise. The Soviets, well aware of this mood, were not shy about pressing their advantages as they consolidated their occupation and control of Eastern Europe.

The State Department Marshall inherited was both terribly disorganized and dominated by a hidebound bureaucracy. To make matters worse, its personnel was scattered throughout some 40 different buildings. Although Marshall seemed to be in unfamiliar surroundings, he had in fact often dealt with many of the people and problems that the State Department encountered daily. Knowing full well that one of his most important jobs was to build a sound command structure, he gathered about him what proved to be the cream of America's talent in the international scene for many years to come. For his chief of staff, he selected Dean Acheson; to head his Policy Plans Division, George F. Kennan; for Russian Affairs, Charles "Chip" Bohlen. Robert Lovett, Will Clayton, Ben Cohen, John Foster Dulles, Dean Rusk, Robert Murphy—all were to serve under him. Such a group seems proof that his instinct for men of mettle and vision could encompass civilians as well as soldiers—and embrace both parties.

To eliminate the administrative chaos, Marshall moved the entire State Department to a single new headquarters—mercifully air-conditioned against the muggy Washington summers. As before, he ruthlessly pruned deadwood. Also as before, he insisted that reports sent to him be boiled down to one page. He told his staff, "Don't fight the problem, decide it . . . I want you to tell *me* what to do." This was a novel and terrifying instruction for those bureaucrats whose skill had been honed in the fine art of evading responsibility. And, as Acheson later recalled, Marshall, recognizing his own lack of experience with the State Department, informed him, " . . . I shall expect of you the most complete frankness, particularly about myself. I have no [personal] feelings except those I reserve for Mrs. Marshall."

Before long a new spirit permeated the department. Charles Bohlen later wrote, ". . . his [Marshall's] personality infected the entire State Department . . . It gave it a sense of direction and purpose. . . . We realized we were working for a great man." Where apathy and indifference had often been the dominant moods, enthusiasm and involvement now prevailed. This was a good thing too, for within weeks of Marshall's arrival, several international crises descended upon him. First was Stalin's new Five-Year Plan, which emphasized production of armaments to "protect the U.S.S.R. against any eventuality." This was a clear reference to the only nation capable of making war on his country: the United States. Then came disclosures of successful Soviet spying on the U.S. atomic weapons program. This was followed by sudden news from Britain that their involvement in combating the Communists in the Greek Civil War was to end in six weeks due to dwindling funds. Their aid to a militarily weak and vulnerable Turkey was to be cut-off for the same reason. Was aid to stop, the fall of Greece would be a foregone conclusion, and the future of Turkey would be jeopardized. Control of Turkey meant control of the Dardanelles—thus direct and free access to the Mediterranean, long a dream of Russian czars and commissars. If the Soviets controlled Turkey, Iran—source of much of the West's oil—was threatened also. Then even the thought of a Russian-controlled India would cease to be unlikely.

Truman agreed to act to thwart the anticipated Soviet onslaught. In a resounding speech he painted the once benevolently portrayed former ally as a sinister giant bent on destroying all that America held dear. In March 1947, a thoroughly shaken Congress agreed to fund the aid program he proposed under the Truman Doctrine. The trouble with the Truman Doctrine was that under its stated terms, " . . . it must be the policy of the United States to support free peoples who are resisting attempted subjugation by armed minorities or by outside pressures," so nearly any country could lay claim to U.S. assistance and intervention. And it obviously stood as a direct challenge to the Soviets.

Marshall was unhappy with the doctrine. He was only too aware that America lacked the muscle to back up Truman's words. Rapid demobilization had gutted U.S. military strength. America might have the atomic bomb, but as an apocalyptic device its use could only be threatened as a last resort—as the Soviets correctly judged.

Flawed as it was, the Truman Doctrine served its purpose for the moment. Europe was reassured that America had not turned completely inward—that it recognized its position as the only other superpower, a position that demanded of it participation in the affairs of other nations. Stalin was put on notice and backed off—at least for a time.

Next came the Foreign Ministers' Conference in Moscow, held in March–April 1947, where a peace treaty with Germany and Austria was the stated objective. The Russians, however, had other ideas, whose basis had been identified by a staffer at the U.S. Embassy in Moscow and transmitted to Washington by cable. Much of what would be foreign policy under Marshall and his successors was to be shaped by what became known as Kennan's Long Telegram.

George Frost Kennan was a young Princeton man, for years posted to the Moscow embassy. In February 1946, he saw an opportunity to convey to an America still infatuated with the Russians a view of them that had not been clearly presented before. In an 8,000-word cable he outlined the causes of Soviet hostility, and what a world shared with them would likely be. Kennan felt that when push came to shove, the Russians would threaten and growl, but stop short of war unless cornered. In his view, the Soviet leadership, like the czars before them, reflected an ancient Russian fear of the West, of being encircled by hostile powers waiting to cut off Russia from the rest of Europe. This stemmed from "the insecurity of an agricultural people trying to live on [a] vast exposed plain in [a] neighborhood of fierce nomadic peoples." He went on:

> It was no mistake that Marxism took root in such a country, for in this dogma, with its basic altruism of purpose, [Lenin, Trotsky, Stalin] found justification for their instinctive fear of [the] outside world, [and] for the dictatorship without which they did not know how to rule . . . In the name of Marxism they sacrificed every single ethical value in their methods and tactics . . . [they are] a political force committed fanatically to the belief that with [the] U.S. there can be no permanent modus vivendi, that it is desirable and necessary [for Russian security] that the internal harmony of our society be disrupted, our traditional way of life be destroyed, and the international authority of our state be broken.

Later, Kennan would add that ironically it was in fact Communism's absolute belief in its ultimate victory that could sometimes make it willing to be rational and open to compromise. But he cautioned that it would require "the adroit and vigilant application of counterforce . . . at every point where they show signs of encroaching upon the interest of a peaceful world."

Marshall had read Kennan's Long Telegram while in China, for on its arrival in Washington the cable had shocked many and had been widely circulated. It had been a major force in Truman's hardening anti-Communist posture, perhaps even the basic reason for the general's mission in China.

At the Moscow Foreign Ministers' Conference, Marshall would have firsthand validation of Kennan's views. Before his departure for Russia, the secretary of state was one of the few in Washington who still believed negotiation with the Soviets was possible. He recognized them as tough and difficult, but his past experiences in successfully dealing with them led him to believe that accommodation was possible. What he was now overlooking was that more than 200 superby armed divisions had stood behind him then, divisions that didn't exist anymore.

World War II had now been over nearly for two years, but its legacy remained more than evident. Germany, and much of Europe, was still littered with ruins. The horrors of Hiroshima and Nagasaki extinguished the last flickers of hope for the Greater East Asia Co-Prosperity Sphere, the Japanese version of Hitler's short-lived 1000-Year Reich. The fearsome armories of Krupp, Brno and Skoda that made the Wehrmacht a superefficient killing machine had been silenced. The German's mightiest efforts seemed dwarfed now, in contrast to the nuclear devastation the Manhattan Project had twice unleashed on Japan. World War II had cost many lives. Germany had lost 4.2 million; Poland even more, with 4.3 million; and Russia, a whopping 20 million. In total, the conflict produced 32 million casualties, including close to half a million Americans. In addition, in the German-engineered Final Solution, 6 million defenseless Jews had been rounded up and slaughtered in a mass genocide. Gypsies, political prisoners, the physically and mentally deficient, homosexuals and thousands and thousands of other "undesirables" had also been exterminated by the Nazis.

It was true that the Nazi specter had been vanquished, but in fact for most of the Allies what followed in victory was ironic. The old European colonial empires—Britain, France, the Netherlands, Belgium (and, of course, Germany and Italy of the Axis Powers)—all had lost or were about to lose their overseas territories—lands that provided them with both, raw materials and controlled markets for their manufactured goods.

It wasn't only the desolation caused by war that brought a somber mood to postwar Europe. The British and French, even though victorious, were exhausted by the war and quietly faded into second-rate powers. The sole possible challenger to U.S. might was Russia. After the initial goodwill and euphoria of victory, this rival was kept at bay only by the American monopoly on nuclear weapons—a monopoly the Soviets were working feverishly to break. Like a phoenix, Russia emerged from the ashes of war incredibly strong—and more than willing to expand its empire. In quick succession it had already swallowed Romania, Albania, Bulgaria, Poland and Yugoslavia. Czechoslovakia seemed destined to be next, and even Austria couldn't be sure of her fate. Yet at home the popular conception was that the United States still reigned supreme and that the loss of those countries hardly mattered.

Marshall and his entourage flew to the Foreign Ministers' Conference in Moscow, joined there by General Mark Clark, military governor of Austria; General Lucius Clay, military governor of the U.S.–occupied zone of Germany; General Walter Bedell Smith, ambassador to Russia; and John Foster Dulles, an observer representing Congress—and the Republican party. The integration of Dulles into Marshall's retinue was later to have far-reaching consequences.

Moscow in March is cold, and while the Soviets had done their best to provide warm accommodations, these fell short of American standards. For six weeks and 43 meetings, the powers discussed Germany's fate and the distribution of spoils of war. The latter was of prime importance to the Russians and French. The Russians were adamant about the Germans paying reparations in the range of 10 billion dollars, and refused to discuss other issues until that one was settled. The fact that Germany was in no position to pay anything at this time did not faze the Russians. Privately, even before leaving Washington, Marshall had stated

The Brandenburg Gate in Berlin came to symbolize the devastation through-out Europe in the years after the war (George C. Marshall Research Library)

he did not expect a peace treaty with Germany to be the outcome, but that he did hope that Austria would be a different story.

Attending the conference were Soviet Foreign Minister Vyacheslav Molotov; British Foreign Secretary Ernest Bevin; French Foreign Minister Georges Bidault; and of course General Marshall. Bidault was in an extremely weak position, for France was racked with Communist demonstrations and violent shows of party strength. Understandably, France had a visceral fear of a strong Germany—both in the military as well as the commercial sense. The French, like the Russians, wanted a gutted Germany, one unable to rise again. Bevin, who as a labor union leader was expected by Marshall to show a pro-Soviet bias, instead looked with deep suspicion on Molotov's proposals. From the Anglo-American perspective, it was desirable to create a weaker federalized German government, one that would be harder to subvert—as opposed to the strong central one the Russians favored.

Earlier, recognizing a commonality of interest, the British and Americans had in effect melded their occupation zones of

Germany, further arousing Soviet suspicions. The French were frightened that the United Kingdom under a Labor government would be likely to nationalize the German coal and steel industries, much of which fell within the British zone and much of which France needed for its own industries. French fears were finally assuaged by Marshall—so at least for the moment, the West was united.

April arrived and the talks continued without much progress on any of the issues discussed. Finally, Marshall sensed that Molotov's goal was simply to stall until the West called the meeting off. This would allow Moscow to use "Western intransigence" for its own propaganda ends. Determined not to let that happen, Marshall decided to call on Stalin himself. On April 15, he met with the Soviet marshal. As usual, his words to Stalin were direct. He told him that the United States was prepared to help rebuild Europe, that it had no intention of dominating any other country and that he would warmly welcome the U.S.-Soviet cooperation that had existed during the war.

A distrustful Stalin replied with a friendly smile that he too would welcome cooperation, but that Germany must first be politically restructured before economic steps could be taken. On the question of reparations, he offered:

> The United States and England might be willing to give up reparations; the Soviet Union cannot. . . . He [Stalin] thinks compromises are possible on all the main questions including demilitarization, political structure for Germany, reparations and economic unity. [But] it is necessary to have patience and not become depressed.

Marshall now began to realize that a weak, starving and disheartened Europe was precisely what Stalin wanted, for an unemployed, unhappy and hungry populace offers the best recruits for Communism.

With the end of the Moscow Foreign Ministers', Conference, the Iron Curtain, a phrase coined by Churchill to describe Soviet containment of Eastern Europe, became a reality. The rift between East and West had crystallized.

Two days after his return from Moscow, toward the end of April 1947, Marshall reported his experiences to the American public in a coast-to-coast radio broadcast. He spoke of his frustration regarding the conference's lack of results. Then he spoke of the need to revitalize Europe, a continent that included 66 million Germans. He described the vital role that German coal and steel played in the economies of other countries. Marshall also addressed the cost to the United States of keeping Germany afloat, a cost that once its industry was restated, Germany itself would assume. Of Stalin's request for patience, he added that time was running out for Europe: "Disintegrating forces are becoming evident. The patient is sinking while the doctors deliberate. So I believe that action cannot await compromise through exhaustion. . . ." Marshall concluded, "The state of the world today and the position of the United States makes mandatory in my opinion unity of action on the part of the American people. It is for that reason that I have gone into such lengthy detail in reporting my views on the conference."

With that speech, the seeds of the Marshall Plan were planted. For months Marshall had been laying the groundwork for such a plan. A joint committee of government authorities had been studying European needs and America's ability to fill them. Marshall recognized that without the backing of Congress he would not be able to accomplish much. He therefore turned to Senator Arthur Vandenberg, the Republican leader, and involved him and the Republican party further in his plans, a move a grateful Vandenberg warmly welcomed.

For Marshall the equation was frighteningly simple. The United States alone now held over 50% of the world's wealth—while the Soviets controlled considerably more than that percentage of the world's armed might. In Germany, the United States had 200,000 men to Russia's 1 million. At home, Marshall doubted he could muster more than a handful of new divisions to the better-than 200 Stalin could additionally command. He did not like engaging in a confrontation without the bayonets to back up his words or at least substantial physical distance from the enemy—a luxury he knew America no longer had. For, as he had put it while still army chief of staff, "For probably the last time in the history of warfare these . . . ocean distances were a vital factor in our defense." To him, Truman's chosen alternative, military dependence on the atomic bomb, was an illusory idea, one predestined to failure.

Marshall saw the solution for long-term world peace not in an armaments race, but in making the people and nations devastated by war strong again. Only the United States was in a position to make that happen. The question was how to make the United States aware that with global supremacy comes global responsibility—that with privilege comes cost. And how could this argument be presented to a nation in the throes of self-congratulation, one determined to forget the war and enjoy the fruits of victory?

An Allied wartime conference in Yalta had divided Europe into two spheres of influence, thus automatically creating an adversarial relationship between the West and the Russians the moment the war was over. It is no wonder then that otherwise sober minds would look with nostalgia upon General Wenkel's offer in the last days of World War II to commit his panzer corps to the allied armies in a preemptive attack on the invading Russians—an offer that when made had been all but inconceivable. And although the West consisted of the democracies of Western Europe, Australia and the Americas, the only nation with the necessary industrial and military might to stand up to the Soviets was in fact the United States.

In the East, the Russians—by virtue of their sheer numbers, doggedness and martial spirit—became at war's end the undisputed rulers of their sphere. Emboldened by their military successes and by strong Communist parties in France, Italy and Greece, the Soviets saw those countries as ripe for the taking too. To that end, Russia flexed her considerable muscles. She eliminated a weak attempt at democracy in Czechoslovakia, threatened to split the Balkans with a civil war in Greece, called for a showdown in Italy and to date was restrained only by the U.S. monopoly on atomic weapons.

The reality was that postwar America had inherited the imperial mantle Rome, Spain and Britain had once worn. Each in its own time ruled supreme, came to decline and in the end surrendered that mantle to a successor. Of them all, America was the only one who had not sought it, the only country in fact willing to cast it away untried—finding even the thought too bothersome. But nations are not like people; they cannot simply abdicate and opt for an easier, simpler life. And nations at the apex carry an additional burden, for others covet that space and will destroy to achieve it. So it was now with Russia. The fearful Soviets would not be satisfied with an American sidestep, for they would interpret such a move as part of some larger deceitful design. The Soviets wanted an America that would not be in a position to harm them. To them this meant a country so weakened by dissension and fear that its own people, dissatisfied with living there, would eventually revolt against their government. Marshall had to bring this Russian vision to the attention of his countrymen and to Congress.

Interestingly enough, Stalin believed that a repeat of the Great Depression was in the making, and that with it America would fall of its own weight; all he needed do was to maintain the pressure. He was right—to the extent that if Western Europe continued its rapid descent unchecked, the United States' own economy, without the external markets that had brought it out of the Depression, would be sucked under too. Marshall had increasingly realized that communism thrives on hunger and discontent, and that a ravaged Europe, left to its own devices, was fertile ground for that dogma. Well aware of the situation's urgency, he anxiously sought an appropriate forum in which to present his plan to Europe. To succeed, though, the message must not alarm Congress nor the U.S. public, but at the same time it must openly and publicly inform the Europeans.

That forum crystallized with Harvard's third offer to him of an honorary degree. He had been too busy to attend their previous commencements, and since the university would not grant the degree in absentia, the occasions had passed. Harvard, the cradle of the establishment, now offered him the right place at the right time for his speech. So when commencement day came on June 5, 1947, a poker-faced Marshall, carrying a panama hat and wearing neither academic robes nor military uniform, led the parade of the day's honorees. Harvard President James B. Conant, in handing him his citation, called him "a soldier and statesman whose ability and character brook only one comparison (George Washington) in the history of the nation."

Marshall's speech that day was brief and poorly read:

> The truth of the matter is that Europe's requirements for the next three or four years . . . are so much greater than her current ability to pay that she must have substantial additional help or face economic, social and political deterioration of a very grave character. . . . The consequences to the economy of the United States should be apparent to all. . . . Our policy is not directed against any country or doctrine but against hunger, poverty, desperation and chaos.

The import of what he was saying was not missed by those most likely to be affected by it, the British and French governments—as well as a puzzled Stalin, who found himself and his satellites included in the offer. Boiled down to its essentials, the Marshall Plan proposed the following:

1. That Europe, including the Soviets, define its own economic problems and solutions.
2. That it do so in concert.
3. That the request each nation brings to the United States for funding be acceptable to the others.
4. That Germany be included.
5. That implementation of the plan involve bilateral agreements between European countries.
6. That the proposals presented be designed to put Europe on its feet within four years.

If the above conditions were met, the United States would underwrite the project to the best of its ability. It would not provide cash but the tools, factories, ships, food, trucks and raw materials needed. To succeed though, the Europeans would have to overcome any distrust and dislike for one another, at least enough to communicate honestly. For instance, France would have to reveal to Britain what materials it lacked. The Belgians would have to talk to the Dutch, the Greeks to the Norwegians, the Austrians to the Italians—and the Germans to everybody.

U.S. coal would restart German and French steel mills until European mines were rebuilt and producing their own. U.S. steel would supply machine tools until these industries recovered. American machinery would jumpstart industrial plants devastated by the war. American foodstuffs would feed the population until the local agriculture could take over.

To a Europe still ravaged from the war, the Marshall Plan offered the only means of salvation. It wasn't just the physical infrastructure—fallen bridges, destroyed railways, bombed-out cities, still-clogged canals, crumbling factories, fields full of unexploded bombs and land mines—that impeded action. The fact was that with nearly every national economy in ruins, money, that vital element for commerce, had lost its value. Inflation soared astronomically. Barter, nylons for soap, chocolates for coal, cigarettes for rent, had taken over. Food shortages, real and contrived, loomed everywhere. Starvation—a word almost unheard of in peacetime Europe since medieval times—became a real possibility, helped by an exceptionally cold winter followed by a disastrous harvest.

America, Australia, Argentina and Canada, the granaries of the modern world, now held nearly all of the Old World's gold reserves. In addition, these countries now had many of Europe's best minds, due to the influx of refugees over the last decade or so. And of these nations, only the United States had the necessary industrial depth, agricultural wealth—and military might—to influence events significantly.

The new idea Marshall presented embodied many of the bitter lessons President Wilson after World War I had failed to foresee, a failure that doomed his vision for the new world. This time, however, the concept was formulated by a stronger leader. It pushed aside French and British fears and insisted on premises as untried as they were bold: Rebuild the economies not only of friends, but of foes; seek not to plunder, but to create.

The first to respond was Ernest Bevin, Britain's foreign minister. He quickly grasped the idea and got the French involved. Molotov grumbled that this was a sinister American plot to dominate the world's economy and rebuffed it—to Marshall's great relief. His gamble had paid off. Were the Soviets to have accepted, it was unlikely that Congress would have considered, never mind funded, the Marshall Plan. But the offer had to have been made. Surprisingly, Soviet-controlled Poland and Czechoslovakia at first agreed to join, but were shortly thereafter forced by the Soviets to change their response.

Next Marshall had to sell his plan to Congress. The price tag was high, for he was asking for $17 billion and wanted a commitment for the full amount up front. In the end a budget of $5.3 billion was approved for the first year. By December 1947, only seven months after the Harvard speech, thanks to Marshall's tireless prodding, the European Recovery Program was launched.

The impact of the plan was quickly felt. As Europeans were fed and their factories and farms began producing, they once again started to trust money, so barter declined and soon disappeared. With money's value accepted, commerce and trade were reestablished. Those who while hungry had embraced communism found that with steady jobs and full bellies the Party's charms were grossly overrated, so they abandoned its ranks by the thousands. The result was the return of political stability. Within three years the nations participating in the Marshall Plan found their standard of living approaching or exceeding the one they had known before the war.

By this generous action, America not only propped up a weakened Europe, but gave itself a period of unparalleled prosperity. Not only had she created a market for her products, but had established commercial relationships that in turn helped to improve her own living standards. The ensuing Pax Americana is today, these many years later, beleaguered by the *economic*—not military—might of America's former enemies. And Soviet communism, once the feared scourge of the Western world, is no more—a feat achieved without a single U.S. soldier having to set foot on Soviet soil.

These are eloquent testaments to the vision of General Marshall.

10

THE END OF THE LINE

Twice in his long career of service, George Marshall shaped U.S. policy to the goals he saw as paramount. First there had been the rearmament and mobilization of the country for World War II; then came the enlightened self-interest and humanitarianism of the Marshall Plan. With both endeavors, his apolitical reputation had been a tool of great power in prodding an unwilling nation to sacrifice in the short term for its best interests in the long term.

In the early years of World War II, America had been indignant at the Nazi invasion of Russia, and did its best to help the Soviets contain and destroy the Wehrmacht's seemingly invincible formations. That same America five years later was asked to look upon the face of what later would be called the "evil empire" and condemn it as the coming of the Antichrist, for by then U.S. perceptions of Russia had drastically changed. The U.S.S.R. had ceased to be the land of stalwart peasants singing as they marched to defend Mother Russia. Now it was seen as a powerful menace, a threat to democratic values and to peace throughout the world.

Postwar Germany had been divided into four zones, each controlled by one of the four former Allied Powers: the United States, Britain, France and the Soviet Union. None of these powers wanted a reunited Germany to fall into the enemy camp.

After the refusal of the Soviets to participate in the Marshall Plan, the West realized eventual political partitioning of Germany into two separate entities was the only solution if aid to that country was to remain a basic building block in the success of the recovery program. Marshall could see that the consolidation of the American, British and French occupation zones would confirm ancient Russian fears of a coalition against them. When to this was added the impact of the Marshall Plan in uniting nearly all the other Western European nations (Spain was excluded)—and U.S. control of Japan, not to mention support of Chiang Kai-shek in China—the Soviets grew enraged and frightened, for they felt the encirclement they had dreaded was now close to complete.

In order to break that choking ring, on June 23, 1948, Stalin ordered the Berlin Blockade. Located one hundred ten miles into the Soviet zone, Berlin had received special status in 1945 and had been *jointly* governed by the four powers since. Besides the Soviet garrison in the city, alert Russian divisions were now quartered within shooting distance, whereas only a few Western batallions were available within the city limits. Stalin was fully aware of his overwhelming conventional-arms superiority. He also knew that the atomic bomb was not likely to be used, for the moral implications of such an act would rend the Western alliance and the American people. So he skillfully maneuvered the crisis, stopping just short of a final fatal step. With the blockade Stalin hoped to demonstrate Russian might and Western impotence—and to stop the consolidation of Germany's other three occupation zones, which he feared would abruptly end his influence on the richer, more industrially advanced sections of the country.

For months the blockade continued. At first it had only been against truck convoys, but then was extended to railway traffic. The Western Allies responded with a massive airlift. Then the Russians declared they would stop all but Soviet flights into the area. But their bluff was called, and after 322 days of the Western Allies airlifting food and fuel into Berlin, the Russians finally gave up. Instead of frightening the West into acceptance of Soviet supremacy, the blockade resulted in the creation of NATO, the North Atlantic Treaty Organization, a defensive alliance pledging military, political and economic cooperation.

In the meantime, Britain had problems in the Near East. By the Balfour Declaration signed in 1917, Palestine was administered under a League of Nations mandate by Britain. That declaration was interpreted by Jews as declaring Palestine a Jewish homeland, so many Jewish settlers made it their home. The Arabs saw the declaration as proposing a joint Jewish-Arab state. In the Holy Land, Arabs numbered some 4 million, Jews less than 400,000. The Arabs had had a long history of tolerance toward the Jews, so the idea of sharing the land was not threatening. However, a Jewish state in what the Arabs also viewed as their own ancestral homeland was entirely another matter.

Two circumstances created a sense of great urgency. The first and perhaps most important was the shadow of the Holocaust, the slaughter of 6 million Jews by the Nazis. There was thus worldwide sympathy for the Zionist movement's goal of creating a nation for the world's displaced Jews. The wartime genocide had generated a great sense of guilt in the Allies, particularly in the United States, which had a large, well-organized and very articulate Jewish population. The second circumstance was the imminent termination of the mandate in May 1948. The British, exasperated by Jewish terrorist activity, and seeing no viable alternative, announced in December 1947 that on May 15, 1948, right on schedule, they would leave Palestine altogether; then Arabs and Jews would be free to solve their problems as they saw fit.

For Marshall, Palestine presented a thorny problem. While he sympathized with the plight of the Jews, he did not see a federalized Arab-Jewish Palestine as a dreadful fate for them. He thought an independent Jewish state could not defend itself against overwhelming Arab odds. To him the whole process seemed futile and would result in the deaths of thousands. In addition Marshall saw that the United States might become involved. Such an involvement would require the deployment of at least 100,000 troops, which the United States did not have. Then there was the matter of oil. The Arab states competed (and still do) with Russia as the prime sources of oil. Would they in their resentment halt its flow? Or worse yet, blow up oil fields?

Consequently, as far as Marshall could see, a Jewish nation was not in the best interest of the United States—his primary concern. His position was that America should neither endorse nor condemn its establishment. Shortly before the vote in the United Nations, Truman summoned Marshall to a final meeting on the subject. The president was lagging behind in the polls for the November 1948 election, so the Jewish vote was more critical than usual for his political future. And American Jewish leaders had made it clear that they would oppose him if the United States voted against the establishment of a Jewish homeland.

After Marshall stated his position, Clark Clifford, the president's political adviser, expressed his support for the idea of a Jewish homeland. Finally, Marshall, judging this advocacy as a purely domestic political concern, exploded in anger. He charged that Clifford's arguments were "a transparent dodge to win a few votes," and then added, "If I were to vote [in the election] I would vote against the President." Years later Clifford would state that after this incident, General Marshall never addressed another word to him.

Truman nevertheless went on to endorse the new nationhood of Israel. He just barely won the presidential election of November 1948. What part the Jewish vote played in that result remains in dispute.

The Marshalls were not in the United States to witness these events, having gone to Europe on what could well have been a conveniently arranged respite. On their return, other pressing issues awaited. There was the continuing Greek civil war; what to do about a disintegrating Nationalist China; and the new French and Italian elections that hopefully would diminish Communist power in those countries. And, of course, there was the Marshall Plan. Katherine returned to Dodona Manor, and Marshall became a weekend commuter to Virginia. To further complicate matters, there were death threats to Marshall from Jewish terrorists who viewed him as the enemy of their budding Israel.

The elections over, Marshall informed Truman that he would resign at the end of the president's first term. But before that time came, the enlarged kidney that had been the ostensible reason for his early summer tour of Europe flared up again. Truman accepted his resignation, and Dean Acheson became the new secretary of state.

Marshall saw Christmas 1948 and New Year's Day 1949 from a bed in Washington's Walter Reed Military Hospital. Get-well wishes poured in from around the world, from such disparate characters as Stalin, de Gaulle, General Albert Wedemeyer, Chiang Kai-shek, Tito, Eisenhower, Queen Frederika of Greece, Mao Zedong, Chaim Weizmann and Churchill.

Marshall recovered, and in September 1949 he returned to public life—this time as head of the American Red Cross. And

Marshall at home with his wife Katherine, and step-daughter and grandchildren (George C. Marshall Research Library)

little more than a year later the phone rang again. Again it was Truman. The call reached him at a village store near a hunting camp. "General, I want you as my Secretary of Defense," Truman insisted. "All right," said Marshall, and hung up, not wanting the half-dozen locals to know what his call had been about.

Things had not been going well in Washington for the Truman administration—even though the president now had a Democratic Congress. The mood of the nation was for peace, and its main concern was with the economy. Instead, there was a war afoot in Korea that no one seemed to want—and for which there were no U.S. troops available because of a greatly reduced U.S. military. Internal dissension was rife, the Department of Defense would not talk to the Department of State; the Joint Chiefs despised their civilian superior and Marshall's predecessor, Secretary of Defense Louis Johnson, who, like Byrnes, had alienated the president. When not fighting Johnson, the Chiefs were tangling over the meager new defense budget. In effect, Marshall was being asked to come to Washington for the thankless job of straightening the mess out. So he accepted the part on the understanding that he would hold it for no more than a year, which he did, almost to the day.

However, Marshall's nomination did not go as smoothly as his one for secretary of state. First there was the matter of his being a soldier. By order of the National Security Act of 1947, the secretary of defense was supposed to be a civilian, not a soldier. Marshall himself had felt it essential that the military have a civilian head. In addition to this hurdle there was vicious partisan opposition.

In a preamble to Joseph McCarthy's own vicious tirades a year later, Republican Senator William Jenner of Indiana opened the debate by attacking Marshall's nomination and impugning Marshall's character. He called the nominee "a coddler of Communism, the man responsible for the loss of Nationalist China, his life a living lie." He added that Marshall was "an errand boy, a front man, a stooge or co-conspirator for this administration's crazy assortment of collectivist cut-throats, and Communist fellow-traveling appeasers."

Then patrician Senator Everett Saltonstall of Massachusetts (also a Republican) stood up and declared,

> If there is any man whose public life has been above censure . . . it is George C. Marshall. I wish I had the vocabulary to answer the statement that the life of George Marshall is a lie, because if ever there was a life spent in the interest of our country, a life that is not a lie, it is the life of George C. Marshall.

One of America's most shameful episodes had begun. But despite attacks such as Jenner's, Marshall's nomination and the amendment to the National Security Act to allow him to serve were passed.

During Marshall's absence from official Washington, the Korean War had begun. Korea, which had been part of Japan since its cession at the end of the Sino-Japanese War of 1894, had been promised independence by the Allies. With World War II over, however, Korea was abruptly divided into North and South, each section occupied respectively by the Soviets and the United States. After 1949's disastrous defeat of the Kuomintang and the victory of Mao Zedong in China, Stalin felt confident enough to instigate North Korea to invade the South on June 24, 1950. The Republic of Korea (ROK) troops, unable to resist the onslaught, retreated in disorder. Korea was not considered a prime American interest, but already George Frost Kennan's limited containment policy was being expanded into a confrontational one by Truman. Marshall opposed this development on the theory that if the United States were to respond to every Soviet attack, it would be surrendering the initiative to the Russians and letting them choose the place and circumstances best suited to their interests. Which is precisely what happened.

Prodded by the Republican right and by his own visceral dislike for communism, Truman saw the North Korean attack as an intolerable Soviet affront and rushed to the aid of South Korea. Luckily, thanks to Stalin's boycott of the United Nations, the United States was able to have the U.N. Security Council pass a resolution condemning North Korea's action—and to make a return to the 38th parallel frontier a U.N. goal. Thus there were not only Republic of Korea and U.S. troops fighting in Korea, but British, Turkish, French and Australian soldiers as well. A total of 15 nations contributed manpower.

This, however, was little consolation for General MacArthur, who was given command of the theater by the United Nations and asked to fight a losing battle with too few troops for a place that seemed to him to be of dubious benefit to his country. Nevertheless, in a brilliant bit of generalship, MacArthur landed troops at Inchon in North Korea while simultaneously pushing up from the port of Pusan in South Korean. By mid-October 1950, he had not only chased the Communists across the 38th parallel, but had also captured North Korea's capital, Pyongyang. The defeat of the enemy was so complete that he decided to carry the battle all the way to the Yalu River, on whose northern bank lay China.

The once-limited objectives, to repel aggression and push the North Koreans back across the 38th parallel, were now superseded with General Marshall's consent. The new objective became control and unification of the whole country under the Seoul government of President Syngman Rhee. But the Chinese, fresh from their victories over the Kuomintang and fearful that America would again intervene in their internal affairs, were determined not to allow Korean reunification. So employing human-wave attacks, Chinese Communist armies entered the fray. The results were disastrous for U.N. forces, which were forced to retreat to the 38th parallel by December 1950.

MacArthur, ever resourceful, organized a counteroffensive, but with an even larger objective than before. He asked for the authority to invade China itself and to use nuclear weapons if necessary. "There is no substitute for victory," he grandly proclaimed—which is quite true—if only military goals are to be satisfied. What MacArthur has seemingly forgotten was Karl von Clausewitz's first axiom: war is an instrument of policy—not an end in itself.

War with China was not only undesirable in that it would not advance U.S. objectives, it could also create a global disaster regardless of outcome. It had not been too many months since the Soviet Union had broken America's nuclear monopoly in 1949. Were an American atomic bomb to be used, the likelihood of retaliation in kind looked quite strong—and with it the arrival of World War III. Not only was the thought intolerable from a moral standpoint, but the United States would once again be caught grossly unprepared for conflict.

So, in spite of his brilliant generalship, MacArthur had to be silenced on matters politic. Orders to that effect came to him first from General Joseph Lawton Collins, the army chief of staff, then from General Omar Bradley and finally from Marshall himself. All this was to no avail. Truman, desperate because MacArthur was a national icon, asked Marshall and the Joint Chiefs for their advice. It was unanimous. MacArthur must go. Truman fired him in April 1951, but in a manner that left a bad taste, even for those who did not have any love for the general. MacArthur learned of his relief from his wife who had heard it on the radio.

Senator Joseph McCarthy, meanwhile, renewed his vicious attacks. And with MacArthur's dismisal, he was given fresh ammunition and opportunity to renew his attacks on Marshall. He did so with increased venom. He read a 60,000-word tirade in the Senate. At first he read to a packed house, but soon the

Senate floor quickly emptied. The gallery did so too, but more slowly. Even *Time* magazine, controlled by "China Lobby" stalwarts and thus hardly a voice of the left, editorialized its disgust with the senator from Wisconsin: "In familiar fashion, McCarthy twisted quotes, drew unwarranted conclusions from the facts he *did* get right, accused Marshall of having made common cause with Stalin since 1943." While this and other sane voices helped, they were becoming fewer. The erosion of America's self-respect had begun. It would take several years for the dreadful scourge of McCarthyism to run its course; there would be many victims. The situation now was not helped by a speech Eisenhower, Marshall's old protege—now running for the presidency—delivered in Wisconsin, McCarthy's home state. As was customary, a written copy had been sent to the press ahead of time.

In the written version Ike had a segment honoring Marshall. But pressured by McCarthy and Wisconsin governor William Kohler, it was dropped in the actual speech. The press picked up on the omission. Even Eisenhower—the soldier, the man whom Marshall had mentored and protected—had been cowed by McCarthy. It seems incredible that America's powerful would not bring McCarthy to task sooner, for they knew him to be a disagreeable liar who boasted of a nonexistent combat record and whose weapons were innuendo, slander and fear.

In September 1951, at the end of the one year to which he had agreed to stay in the post, Marshall resigned as secretary of defense. In one of his many efforts to amend his former lapse, Eisenhower invited Marshall to his presidential inauguration in January 1953 as one of the most important guests. When White House dinners were held for visiting heads of state, Marshall was included more often than not. And later he would represent President Eisenhower and the United States in London at the coronation of Elizabeth II on June 2, 1953.

Perhaps Marshall's greatest honor is one no other soldier has attained. Marshall was selected as the 1953 winner of the Nobel Peace Prize. At the ceremonies in Oslo on December 10, just as he was about to be decorated, demonstrators in the balconies shouted, "Murderer, murderer," referring to his role in Hiroshima and Nagasaki. At this, King Haakon of Norway rose and applauded Marshall. The entire audience joined in and gave Marshall a standing ovation, drowning out the demonstrators.

Marshall had gone to Norway in poor health, and the trip did not improve it. From this point on, his health declined rapidly. Slowly at first, his faculties began to weaken. His incipient deafness increased, and his memory faltered. Stroke followed stroke. More and more his home became a room at Walter Reed Hospital.

Weeks passed, and Marshall, now 79, remained hospitalized in Washington. At his bedside appeared a long parade of notables, men and women whom he had met or worked with over a long and fruitful life. In person, by mail and telephone, friends and acquaintances did their best to cheer him. There was Queen Frederika of Greece, with whom he carried a long and intimate correspondence. There was Chiang Kai-shek's wife, Soong Mei-ling, the "Dragon Lady" of China, who called him General Flicker, his childhood nickname. There were Winston Churchill, Dwight D. Eisenhower, Harry Truman and Dean Acheson and his aide and factotum Sergeant Powder. Rose Page, his goddaughter, and Molly, his step-daughter, visited, but he could hardly recognize them. Always nearby was his wife, Katherine.

On October 16, 1959, George Catlett Marshall of the Marshalls of Virginia died. America had not only lost a great general and statesman, but also a friend who embodied its best qualities.

After the shameful years of McCarthy had passed, an unsure America began to recover its pride when a young president, mindful of the past, demanded of his citizens, "Ask not what your country can do for you—ask what you can do for your country." To the Marshalls of this world, the response to that challenge has never been in doubt.

EPILOGUE

The world we live in today and the peace we enjoy have been shaped in large measure by the life and work of George C. Marshall. True, conflicts have since erupted in many places, but no general conflagrations on the order of the last two world wars have occurred. For several decades the democracies lived under the shadow of a potential Soviet threat, one that would long ago have been a reality without the Marshall Plan. The plan's foresight in building up victor and vanquished alike created a bulwark that stopped the Communist tide without the need for a single U.S. soldier to cross the Soviets' frontiers. That the plan in so doing benefited the United States enormously also speaks to its credit. Marshall both conceived it and convinced a doubting and isolationist America of its necessity. It was in recognition of these accomplishments that Marshall was awarded the Nobel Peace Prize, the first and only soldier to be so honored.

Earlier still, with the advent of World War II, another global threat had arisen, one that had caught the United States totally unprepared. It was arguably only British pluck, Marshall's untiring efforts to rearm the country and the incredible resources of America that managed to stop the Nazi tide.

Marshall was a man of whom Roosevelt would later say, "General, I could not rest easy with you out of Washington." Joseph Stalin, a man not given to trusting anyone, insisted, "I would trust General Marshall with my life." President Truman called him "the greatest living American." And Churchill referred to him as "the organizer of victory."

The accolades were innumerable as befits a hero, but many of them spoke not only to his achievements, but to his personal greatness. In an age tinged with cynicism, it is indeed a marvel to find a man unwilling to compromise ideals for advancement; one who can acknowledge his mistakes without recourse to excuse or scapegoat; one willing to subordinate his needs to those of his country. Though a southerner by ancestry and choice, in many ways the general was also the archetypal

Yankee—a man of great modesty, few words, granite willpower and deeply held beliefs—the quintessential patriot. Like George Washington, to whom he was compared, he sought to unify, not divide; to lead by creating trust, not fear; to exhort by example, not by harangue.

Perhaps the accolade that Marshall the soldier would have liked best came from another general, Matthew Ridgway: "The combat soldier never had a better friend . . . he never forgot the man with the rifle. The man whose task it was to kill or be killed."

CHRONOLOGY

December 31, 1880	George Catlett Marshall, Jr., born, Uniontown, Pennsylvania
September 1897– June 1901	Educated at Virginia Military Institute (VMI); graduates as first captain
February 2, 1902	Commissioned second lieutenant of infantry, U.S. Army
February 11, 1902	Marries Elizabeth Carter Coles
May 1902– November 1903	Serves in the Philippines
December 1903– August 1906	Sees duty in Oklahoma and Texas
August 1906– July 1908	Student, Army Service School and Staff College, Fort Leavenworth, Kansas
March 1907	Promoted to first lieutenant
June 1908–1910	Appointed instructor, Army Service School and Staff College
September 1912	Posted to Fourth Infantry Regiment, Arkansas, Massachusetts and Texas
August 1913– May 1916	Posted to the Philippines
October 1916	Promoted to captain
April 1917	United States enters World War I
June 1917– November 1918	Serves in World War I in France as assistant chief of staff, First Army

November 1918	Armistice ending World War I
May 1919–1924	Aide-de-camp to General John J. Pershing, in France and in Washington, D.C.
July 1920	Promoted to major
August 1923	Promoted to lieutenant colonel
September 1924	Posted to Fifteenth Infantry Regiment, Tientsin, China
July 1927	Posted as instructor, Army War College, Washington, D.C.
September 15, 1927	Elizabeth Coles Marshall dies
October 1927	Posted to Infantry School, Fort Benning, Georgia
October 1929	Stock market crash; Great Depression begins
October 15, 1930	Marries Katherine Tupper Brown
September 1933	Promoted to colonel
October 1933	Instructor, Illinois National Guard, Chicago
October 1936	Promoted to brigadier general
October 1936	Brigadier general and commandant, Fifth Brigade of the Third Division, Vancouver Barracks, Washington
October 1938	Promoted to deputy chief of staff of the army, Washington, D.C.
September 1939	German invasion of Poland; World War II begins
April–July 1940	Germany conquers Denmark, Norway, Holland, Belgium, Luxembourg and France; British evacuate Dunkirk; Battle of Britain

September 1940	First peacetime draft in U.S. history initiated, Japan moves into Indochina and joins Axis powers
March 11, 1941	Lend-Lease Act passed by Congress
April–June 1941	Germany invades the Balkans and the Soviet Union
December 7, 1941	Japanese attack Pearl Harbor
December 1941– January 1942	Arcadia Conference and formation of Grand Alliance
January 1943	Casablanca Conference; Allies announce they will accept only the unconditional surrender of the Axis powers
October–December 1943	Moscow-Cairo-Teheran conferences; Operation Overlord reaffirmed with Eisenhower as commander
January 1944	Selected *Time*'s Man of the Year
May 1944	Marshall's stepson Allen Tupper Brown dies in Italy
June 1944	Rome captured by Allies; Operation Overlord launched
October 1944	Stilwell recalled from China; invasions of the Philippines; by U.S. forces; Battle of Leyte Gulf
December 1944	Appointed general of the army with five stars; German offensive in the Ardennes (Battle of the Bulge)
February 1945	Yalta Conference delineates postwar spheres of influence
April 12, 1945	Roosevelt dies
May 7, 1945	Germany surrenders

August 1945	Atomic bombs dropped on Hiroshima and Nagasaki; Japan surrenders
November 1945	Retires as chief of staff; appointed special envoy to China
January 1947	Recalled from China and appointed secretary of state
March–April 1947	Moscow Foreign Ministers' Conference; Truman Doctrine
June 1947	Marshall Plan speech at Harvard University
January 1948	Second selection as *Time*'s Man of the Year
June 23, 1948	Berlin Blockade begins
July–December 1948	Berlin airlift and counterblockade
January 1949	Resigns as Secretary of State
1949	Appointed head of American Red Cross
1949	Chiang flees China mainland
June 24, 1950	Korean War begins
September 1950	Appointed secretary of defense
September 1951	Resigns as secretary of defense and retires
November 1952	Eisenhower elected president
December 10, 1953	Awarded Nobel Peace Prize
October 16, 1959	Dies at Walter Reed Army Hospital

BIBLIOGRAPHY

The best source of material on the life of General Marshall is the four-volume work by Forrest C. Pogue, his official biographer. Indeed, it has been the primary resource for most accounts of Marshall's accomplishments—and for most of the quotations noted in this volume. Dr. Pogue personally tape-recorded many hours of interviews with the general and has in effect made this biography his life's effort. The army, of course, has extensive archives on Marshall, as does the George C. Marshall Foundation and Library, whose first director was Dr. Pogue. The foundation is located in Lexington, Virginia, at the site of Marshall's alma mater, the Virginia Military Institute. Three other works on the general and his times deserve special mention. These include Ed Cray's *General of the Army George C. Marshall, Soldier and Stateman;* Mark A. Stoler's *George C. Marshall, Soldier-Stateman of the American Century;* and Thomas Parrish's *Roosevelt and Marshall, Partners in Politics and War.* Newspapers and magazines of the period abound with stories about the general. Four particularly rich sources are the great news magazines of the era, *Time* and *Life,* as well as the *New York Times* and the *Washington Post.* Below are a number of volumes that deal with men whose lives the general influenced, and specific events, times or issues on which he had great impact.

Acheson, Dean. *Present at the Creation: My Years in the State Department.* W. W. Norton, New York, 1969.

Alperovitz, Gar. *Atomic Diplomacy: Hiroshima and Potsdam.* Elisabeth Sifton Books, Penguin Books, New York, 1985.

Anderson, Jack, and May, Ronald W. *McCarthy: The Man, the Senator, the "Ism."* Beacon Press, Boston, 1952.

Chinnock, Frank W. *Nagasaki: The Forgotten Bomb.* World Publishing, New York, 1969.

Clarke, Thurston. *Pearl Harbor Ghosts: A Journey to Hawaii Then and Now.* William Morrow, New York, 1991.

Cray, Ed. *General of the Army George C. Marshall, Soldier and Statesman*. W. W. Norton, New York, 1990.

Djilas, Milovan. *Conversations with Stalin*. Harcourt, Brace & World, New York, 1962.

Gilbert, Martin. *The Second World War: A Complete History*. Henry Holt, New York, 1988.

Hodgson, Godfrey. *The Colonel: The Life and Wars of Henry Stimson 1867–1950*. Alfred A. Knopf, New York, 1990.

Honan, William H. *Visions of Infamy*. St Martin's Press, New York, 1991.

Ismay. *The Memoirs of General Lord Ismay*. Viking Press, New York, 1960.

Kennan, George F. *Memoirs*. 2 vols. Little, Brown, Boston, 1967–1972.

Kennett, Lee. *For the Duration . . . The U.S. Goes to War*. Charles Scriber's Sons, New York, 1985.

Kurzman, Dan. *Day of the Bomb—Countdown to Hiroshima*. McGraw-Hill, New York, 1986.

Lash, Joseph P. *Roosevelt and Churchill 1939–1941: The Partnership That Saved the West*. W. W. Norton, New York, 1976.

Lewin, Ronald. *Ultra Goes to War*. McGraw-Hill, New York, 1978.

MacArthur, Douglas. *Reminiscences*. McGraw-Hill, New York, 1964.

Markl, Julia. *Turning Points of World War II: The Battle of Britain*. Franklin Watts, New York, 1984.

Marshall, George C. *Memoirs of My Services in the World War, 1917–1918*. Houghton Mifflin, Boston, 1976.

Mee, Charles L., Jr. *The Marshall Plan: The Launching of the Pax Americana*. Simon & Schuster, 1984.

Mosley, Leonard. *Marshall: Hero for Our Times*. Hearst Books, New York, 1982.

Murphy, Robert. *Diplomat Among Warriors*. Pyramid Books, New York, 1965.

O'Connor, Richard. *Black Jack Pershing*. Doubleday, New York, 1961.

Parrish, Thomas. *Roosevelt and Marshall: Partners in Politics and War*. William Morrow, New York, 1989.

Pogue, Forrest C. *George C. Marshall: Education of a General, 1880–1939; Ordeal and Hope, 1939–1942; Organizer of Vic-

tory, 1943–1945; and *Statesman, 1945–1959.* Viking Press, New York, 1963–1986.

Shapiro, William E. *Turning Points of World War II: Pearl Harbor.* Franklin Watts, New York, 1984.

Shirer, William L. *The Rise and Fall of the Third Reich.* Simon & Schuster, New York, 1960.

Stoler, Mark A. *George C. Marshall, Soldier-Statesman of the American Century.* Twayne Publishers of G. K. Hall & Co., Boston, 1989.

Sukai, Sakur. *Samurai!* E. P. Dutton, New York, 1957.

Thomas, Gordon, and Witts, Max Morgan. *Enola Gay.* Stein & Day, New York, 1977.

Tuchman, Barbara. *Stilwell and the American Experience in China, 1911–1945.* Macmillan, New York, 1970.

Tuchman, Barbara W. *The Guns of August.* Dell Publishing, New York, 1963.

Vandiver, Frank E. *Black Jack: The Life and Times of John J. Pershing.* 2 vols., Texas A&M University Press, College Station, Texas, 1977.

Wedemeyer, Albert C. *Wedemeyer Reports* Henry Holt, New York, 1958.

White, Theodore H. *In Search of History: A Personal Adventure.* Harper & Row, New York, 1978.

White, Theodore H., Ed. *The Stilwell Papers.* William Sloan Associates, New York, 1948.

INDEX

Italic numbers indicate illustrations; a *c* following a page number indicates mention in the Chronology.